# DEFINE

# FINE

## HONG KONG

# DEFINE FINE

## OUR PERSONAL
# INDEPENDENT
## GUIDE

## UNIQUE
### PLACES, PRODUCTS, PEOPLE

# DEFINE FINE
## SUPPORTS

# ONLY

PRIVATELY OWNED BUSINESSES
AND
INDEPENDENT ENTREPRENEURS

# DEFINE FINE

## is OUR PERSONAL COLLECTION of

### PLACES WE LOVE

Dear reader,

We are delighted that you are holding one of our Define Fine travel books in your hands. This book is a result of our very personal and very careful research of the life of this amazing city. It is also a result of very long walks, many sleepless nights and early mornings, heated discussions and our passion for everything beautiful.

In this book you will not find the usual selection of big hotels and famous sights, those you already know or will discover without difficulty on your own or in other guides. We are offering you a selection of places we personally love, the best that this city and its people have to offer - the places that the locals consider to be special, the places they love and are proud of. We are grateful for their guidance and recommendations. But ultimately this is our and very personal choice of the finest of privately owned and operated businesses, in all spheres of life and all price ranges. Being entrepreneurs ourselves we made it our mission to support and promote projects which have unique esthetical value.

We are travelling the world with our eyes and hearts wide open to beauty in all its manifestations. We are delighted to share with you the treasures we found on the way. We do believe that your travel through this city guided by us will be exciting, enchanting, enriching. We are not claiming this selection to be final, there are always new places to discover. But we are sure that we can guide you to what a world traveller should experience – the essence of Hong Kong.

Enjoy your trip!

Veronika Blomgren        Nikola Kostic

# CONTENT

- 16 | City
- 28 | Rooms
- 48 | Food
- 100 | Art
- 116 | Fashion
- 134 | Interior Design and Décor
- 154 | Health and Beauty
- 170 | Adventure

# PLACES BY CITY AREAS

## CENTRAL

| | |
|---|---|
| The Putman | 34 |
| The Jervois | 36 |
| Hotel LKF by Rhombus | 38 |
| Madera Hollywood | 42 |
| The Pottinger | 40 |
| Mana! | 70 |
| Vom Fass | 56 |
| Safe Bubbles&Malt | 54 |
| Sepa | 62 |
| Posto pubblico | 68 |
| Aberdeen Street Social | 66 |
| Tivo Wine Bar | 58 |
| The Woods | 52 |
| Naked Gurume Gyarari | 60 |
| Butchers Barrel | 86 |
| The Monogamous Chinese | 84 |
| PMQ | 120 |
| Initial | 130 |
| Woaw | 122 |
| Lianca | 124 |
| Markin | 126 |
| Jimlly Jewelry | 128 |
| Greenfingers' Academy | 138 |
| Home Essentials | 140 |
| Tequila Kola | 150 |
| Tree | 152 |
| La Galerie | 104 |
| Opera Gallery | 106 |
| Agnes b's Librairie Galeries | 108 |
| Art Beatus | 110 |
| Gecko Lounge | 112 |
| Sin Sin Fine Art | 114 |
| Hong Kong Zoological and Botanical gardens | 158 |
| The Strand | 160 |
| Beyorg | 162 |
| Gentlemen's Tonic | 164 |
| Fox and The Barber | 168 |
| Aqualuna Junk Boat | 174 |
| Timothy Oulton | 142 |

## SHEUNG WAN

| | |
|---|---|
| 99 Bonham | 44 |
| Vasco&Isono | 72 |
| Bibo | 74 |
| Teakha | 78 |
| Hollywood Road | 144 |

| | |
|---|---|
| Amelie & Tulips | 146 |
| Ray Chan Hair Salon | 166 |
| Hong Kong Museum of Medical Science | 180 |

## CAUSEWAY BAY
| | |
|---|---|
| Lanson Place | 46 |
| Loveramics | 148 |

## WAN CHAI
| | |
|---|---|
| 22 ships | 92 |
| Ham & Sherry | 90 |
| The Pawn | 88 |
| Timothy Oulton | 142 |

## REPULSE BAY
| | |
|---|---|
| Hotshot | 94 |

## ADMIRALTY
| | |
|---|---|
| Upper House | 32 |

## TSIM SHA TSUI
| | |
|---|---|
| Aqua | 64 |
| Hutong | 80 |
| Wooloomooloo Prime | 82 |
| Above & Beyond | 98 |

## TAI PING SHAN
| | |
|---|---|
| Brothers Leathercraft #50 | 132 |

## STANLEY
| | |
|---|---|
| The Boathouse | 96 |

| | |
|---|---|
| Stanley | 176 |
| Big Wave Bay | 178 |
| Repulse Bay | 182 |
| Lamma Island | 184 |
| Shek O | 186 |
| Helicopter Tour | 188 |

CITY

some call it the New York of Asia. Others say it reminds them of Europe, and the rest would admit this city is unlike any other. Hong Kong is a clash of cultures and a mismatch of subcultures. It's pretty much like a dim sum stuffing: you're never quite sure what's in the mix, but it tastes bloody good and you always crave more.

Yes, we are talking about food right away and we have a solid reason for that; if New York is the city that never sleeps, then Hong Kong is the city that always eats! This might be a cliché but it's so true that you can't – and you definitely shouldn't – avoid it! Well, Hong Kong never sleeps either. This city has that young vibe that is almost vocalised: it waltzes you and spins you, and makes you sha-la-la, all day and all night long.

Clichés aside, Hong Kong can be viewed through a dozen lenses. It can be exotic or familiar, extremely 'oriental' or mellow European, dynamic and sleepy, urban and "villagy", traditional and so-hip-it-hurts – sometimes all of the above at the very same time. That's probably the reason why it's hard to find a person who won't be impressed by this beauty – this city has the key to anyone's heart and it's not shy to use it.

You can spend days and days wandering in the asphalt jungle of the HK island, sipping on the cocktails at the rooftop bars and exploring the foodie paradise that this city is… or you can sail away and discover a different universe of stunning nature, sandy shores and sleepy fishermen's villages. You can splurge in the most exquisite boutiques in the morning, and then spend an afternoon surfing and enjoying your sunset BBQ, barefoot. You can party all-night-long and hang with South Eastern Asia's coolest cats, and then spend the next day exploring the stalls with traditional Chinese healing herbs in the streets, that look like they belong to the past, past century.

One thing you won't experience here is boredom! That we can guarantee for sure.

ROOMS

Let's get it out of the way quickly: Hong Kong is not exactly famous for its spacious accommodation. Being one of the most expensive places to live in, this vertical jungle can be a challenge for those looking for a proper-sized apartment or a hotel room that won't break the bank. Not to worry though, you won't spend much time in it, as you simply won't have enough time! More good news to follow: the modest sized accommodation is compensated for, with a pretty good choice of boutique hotels, nice location for the city apartments and a creative approach in general. You could pick a design hotel in the heart of the city and enjoy the privacy of your sleek and modern suite, with a panoramic view of course. Or alternatively, you could stay in a nice flat overlooking the bay and live the life of a local expat grilling steaks you've bought in a nearby gourmet supermarket, and having a glass of wine on your own balcony – and you will need some remedy to fight that inevitable vertigo. Trust us!

ROOMS

Area: ADMIRALTY
Pacific Place, 88 Queensway

# THE UPPER HOUSE

Sleek, minimalistic and très chic. Unobstructed harbour panorama. Bathroom with that view. REN toiletries – as lux as can be. You won't be in the centre of the tourist whirlpool while staying here, but the spacious, airy suites – in sharp contrast with "normal" claustrophobic accommodation (typical for Hong Kong) – are worth the compromise. The Upper House is also famous for its restaurant, Café Gray Deluxe, run by celebrity chef Gray Kunz, which attracts a very elegant crowd – look in for a glass of blood orange mimosa, high tea, scrumptious dinner or an epic Sunday brunch, and blend in with the citizens in the know.

www.upperhouse.com

ROOMS

Area: CENTRAL
202 Queen's Road

# THE PUTMAN

The purist's heaven: it's all white and flawless! The grand dame of the modern French interior design Andrè Putman, whom we adore, is in charge, and you can feel her signature Parisienne touch in every corner of this chic boutique apartment hotel. It's classy yet cosy and inviting – exactly how you'd like your home away from home to be like.

www.theputman.com

THE PUTMAN

ROOMS

Area: CENTRAL
89 Jervois Street

# THE JERVOIS

God is in the details: The Jervois might appear yet another minimalistic, white hotel at first sight, but the little things – the scarlet bed throw, the funky artwork on the wall, the play of textures, the collectable coffee table books – give away its coolness. That's what happens when two Frenchmen are in charge! We wish one of the suites could be our long-term residence in Hong Kong.

www.thejervois.com

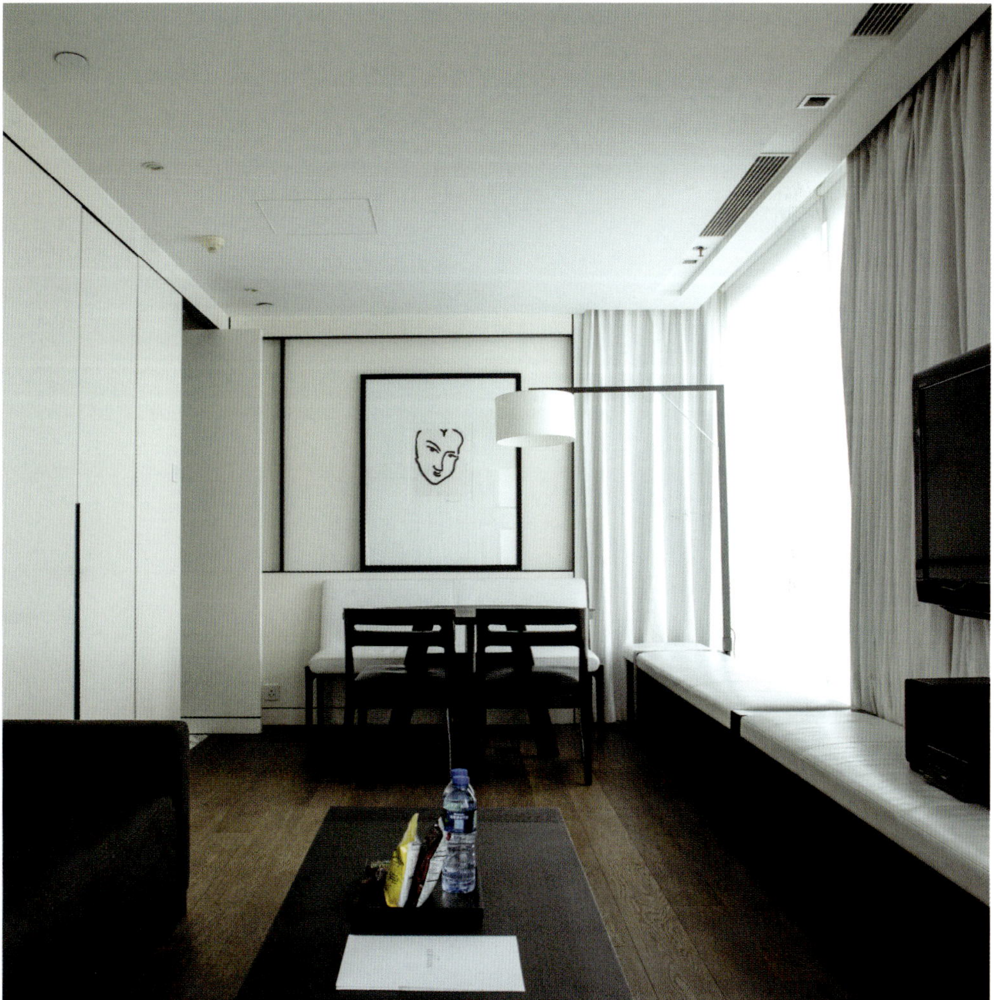

ROOMS

Area: CENTRAL
33 Wyndham Street, Lan Kwai Fong

# HOTEL LKF
## by Rhombus

The party hub! Who cares about the rooms (although they are very nice) when you can go to a handful of the city's coolest bars and restaurants without even leaving the building? Have you been dancing the night away and falling off your stilettos? Press the lift button and go directly to your bed.

www.hotel-lkf.com.hk

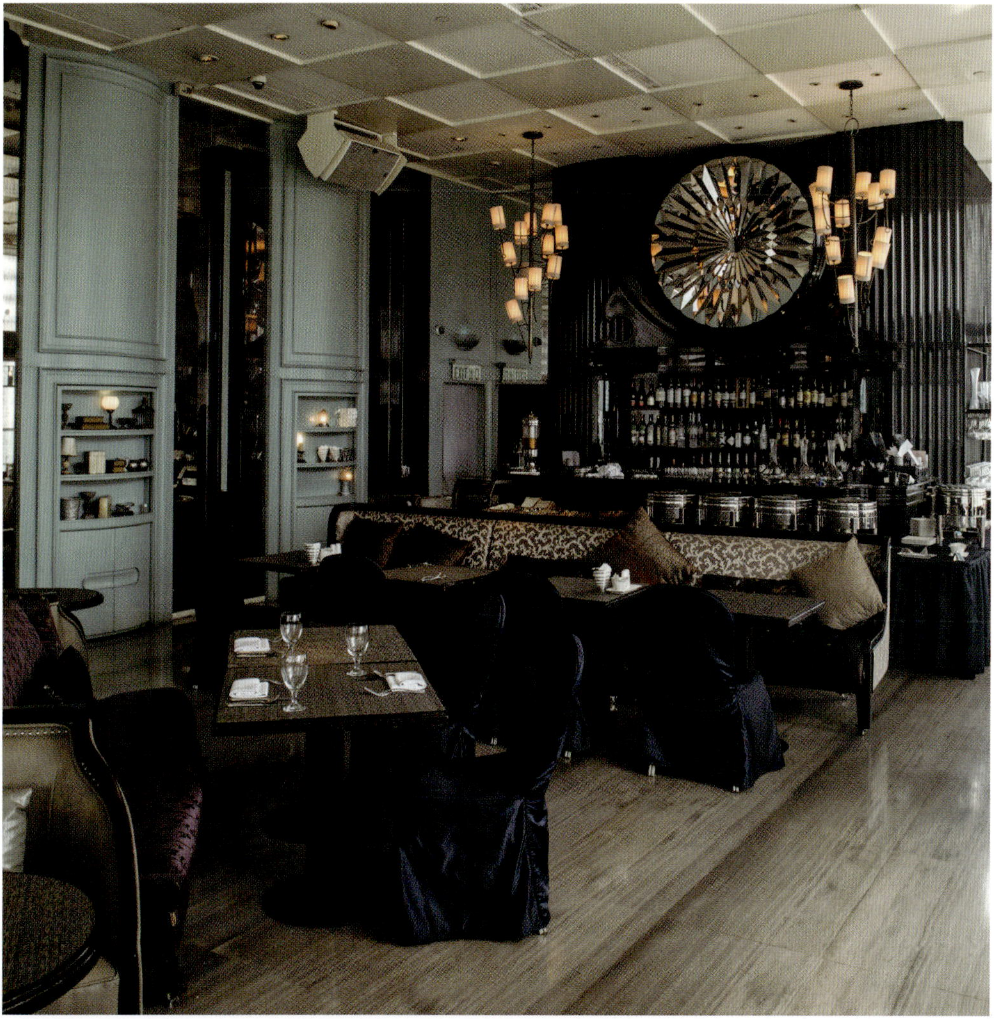

ROOMS

Area: CENTRAL
74 Queen's Road

# THE POTTINGER

Prettier than an antique lacquer box, this hi-end boutique hotel is packed with history, style and gossiping socialites. Named after the first British governor, The Pottinger is glam, not to say posh. You won't find the rooms amazingly spacious but that surely will be atoned with the brisk service, kind attention of the staff wrapped in crispy uniform and the hotel's restaurant Gradini as well as The Envoy's bar.

www.thepottinger.com

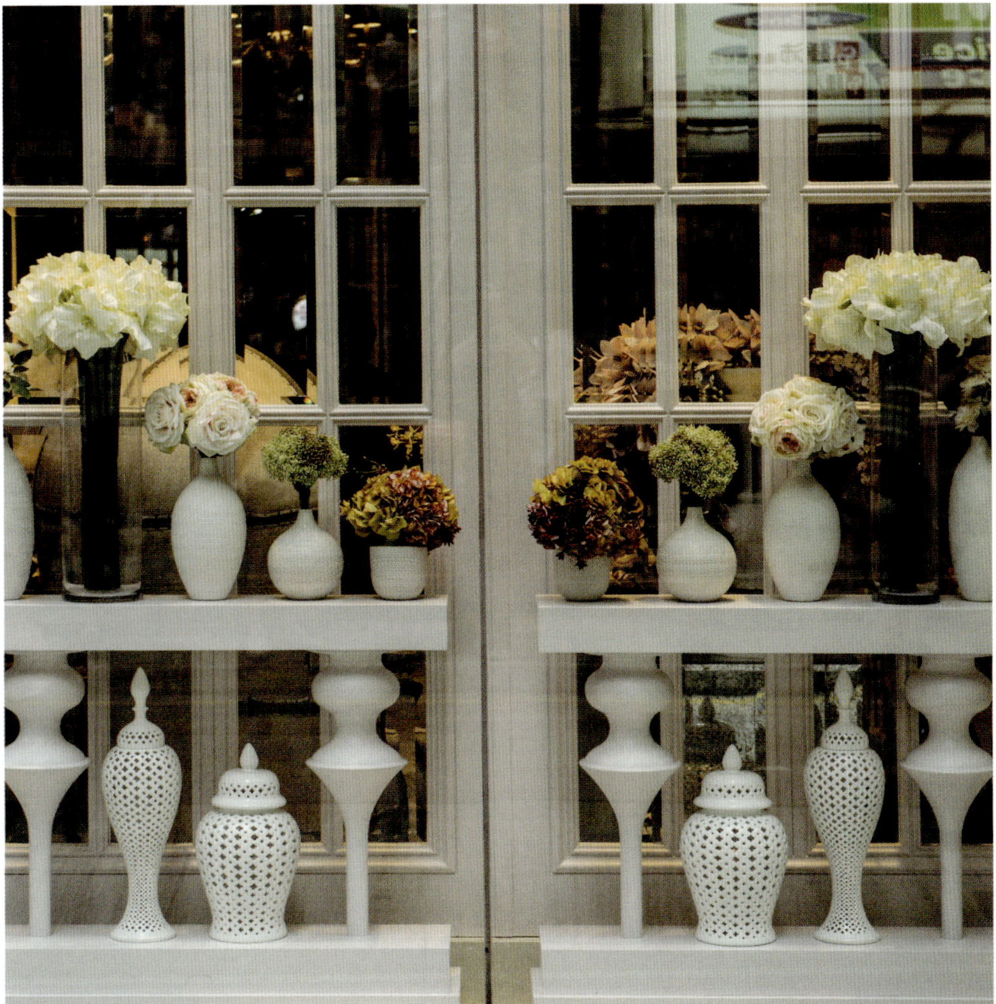

ROOMS

Area: CENTRAL
53-55 Hollywood Road

# MADERA HOLLYWOOD

Are you team Marilyn Monroe or team Charlie Chaplin? This brand new boutique hotel exploits the retro Hollywood glitz like a blonde starlet and her middle-aged admirer. The rooms burst with colours, the retro details look playful in the modern setting and there are some precious little secrets to discover – like Chaplin's personal belongings bought at auction. A perfect piece of Hollywood glamour in the middle of Hollywood road!

www.maderagroup.com/hollywood

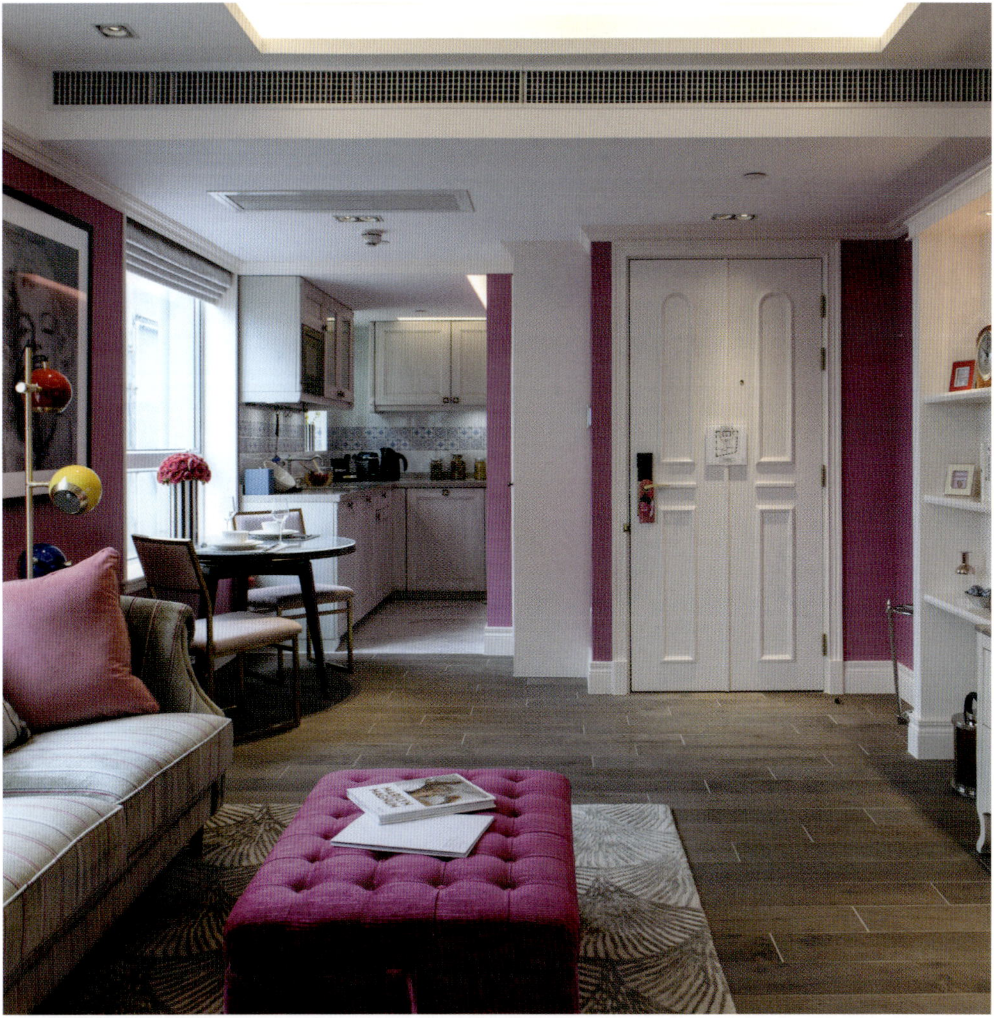

ROOMS

Area: SHEUNG WAN
99 Bonham Strand

# 99 BONHAM

Hong Kong skyline peeking in your bedroom windows? Yes, please! Check in into one of the New York inspired lofts: 50 shades of grey, über-urban décor…just lift the blinds and let the city in. That's how we would like our long-term Hong Kong shelter: a hip, not too touristy location, ideal proximity to everything in the city, and high-class facilities for an honest price. And yes, the bathtub. Thank you very much!

www.99bonham.com

99 BONHAM

ROOMS

Area: CAUSEWAY BAY
133 Leighton Road

# LANSON PLACE

Cool shades, soft lines, exquisite textiles, grand piano and Murano chandeliers – this boutique hotel mimics a 19th century Paris mansion. A charming accommodation in the middle of shopping central.

www.hongkong.lansonplace.com

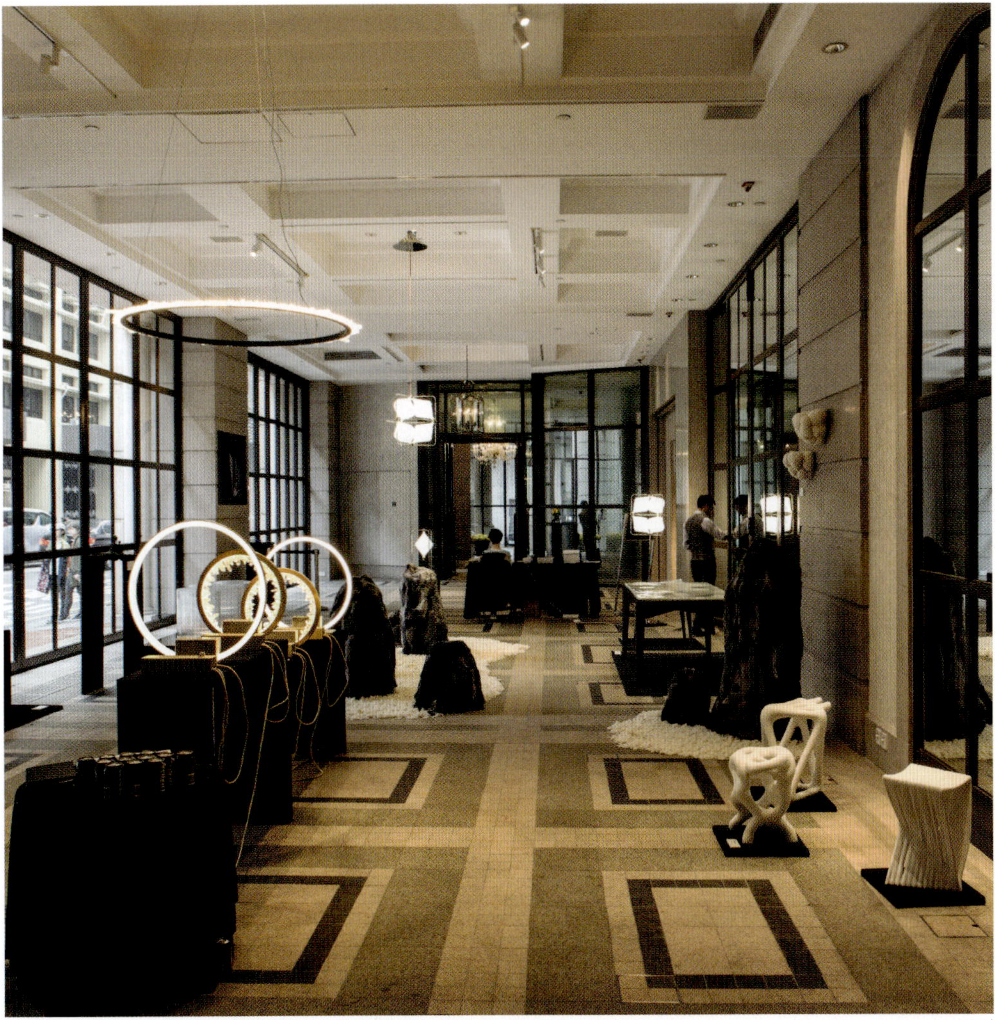

FOOD

Pack some oversized clothes for your Hong Kong trip, as you'll surely gain some extra kilos, and we can assure you that it will happen pretty quickly. Hong Kong eats like there is no tomorrow, and everything goes: dim sums, burgers, roasted geese, steaks, oysters. This is the place where Spanish meets Thai, French blends with Mexican, and traditional Cantonese marries modern fusion. You won't starve in this city. Oh no! In fact, you'll be constantly torn apart with a variety of choices: should you dine at yet another brand new venue, open by yet another celebrity chef, or go for grease (but fun) street food or check out that primitive-looking canteen at the corner that apparently has a Michelin star? Whatever you choose, get ready for the pre-dinner snack and some post-dinner treats, too. Don't even think of stepping on those scales at the end of this trip! It's a tough life to be a Hong Kong foodie. Don't tell us you haven't been warned.

耀發海鮮

YIU FAI

耀昌海鮮 5417

FOOD

Area: CENTRAL
L/G, 17-19 Hollywood Rd

# THE WOODS

Into the woods of the gourmet drinking experience we go! We love the idea of having the seasonal veggies and fruits on our plates, but in the glasses…? That's something fresh indeed! Pair your vodka with mustard seeds, dill and pickles, your gin with young beetroot, your aged rum with toasted cumin and fresh carrot juice. Spiced pumpkin latte…sorry, margarita? Why not, if it's the proper season!

www.thewoods.hk

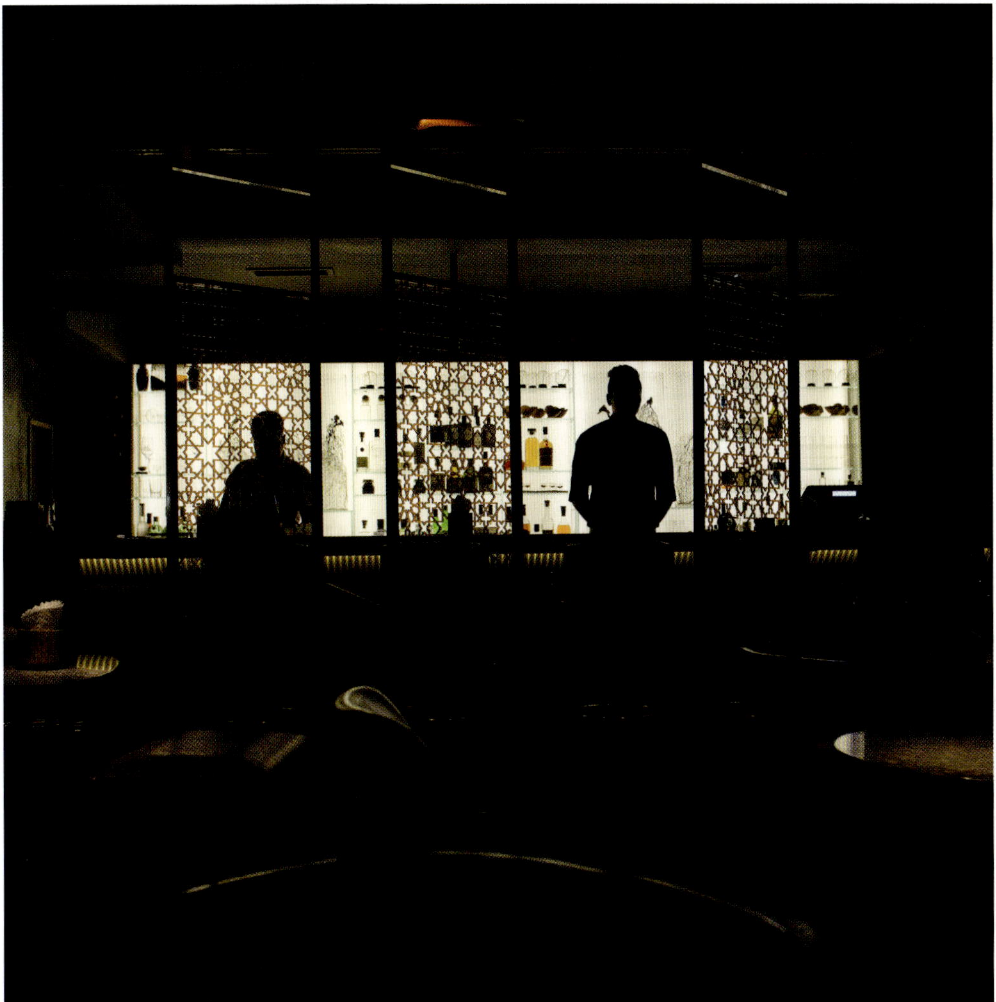

FOOD

Area: CENTRAL
Shop 2, 255 Queen's Rd C

# SAFE
# BUBBLES&MALT

700 kinds of whiskey and 200 sorts of bubbly – whoa, you really need that bulletproof door to keep it safe as it would be in a…safe! You can sip on your favorite spirit at the shiny bar while observing the crowd or hide in one of a private nooks and get naughty – get another bottle and maybe dance on a table, 'cause it's Hong Kong, baby! Although the bar set up is sexy, it's all about the door, really: when you see it, you really, really want to find out what's behind. So press that secret button and enjoy your adventure!

www.smws.com.hk

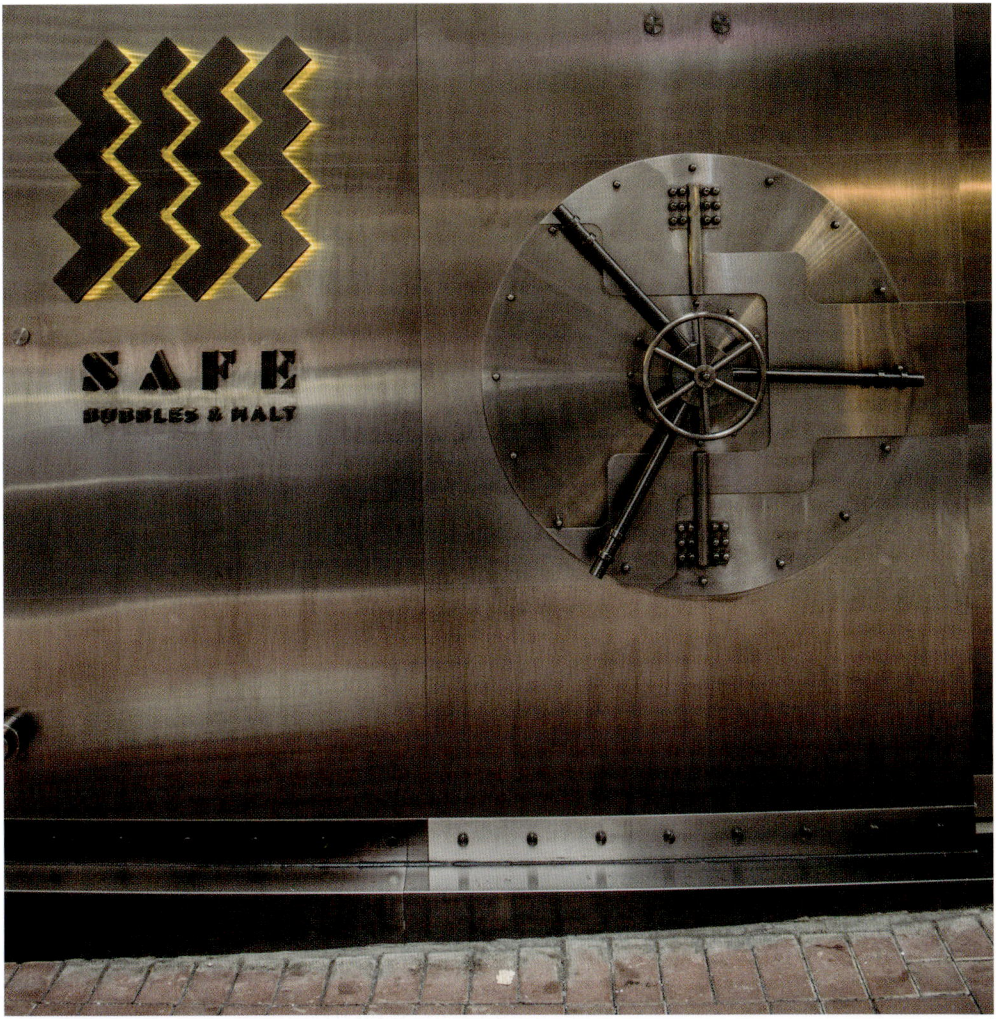
SAFE
BUBBLES & MALT

FOOD

Area: CENTRAL
68A Hollywood Road

# VOM FASS

White Truffle Oil, Forest Raspberry Balsamic vinegar and a zillion other 100% pure and 300% delish oils and vinegars plus gourmet liquers, vintage wines, rare whiskeys – welcome to the candy shop for grown up foodies! 20 years of experience speak for themselves – two brothers behind this project know exactly what excites a picky gourmand. Trust us, you won't leave empty-handed even if your cupboard is already stuffed with everything one might need and your luggage is getting critically overweight!

www.vomfass.com.hk

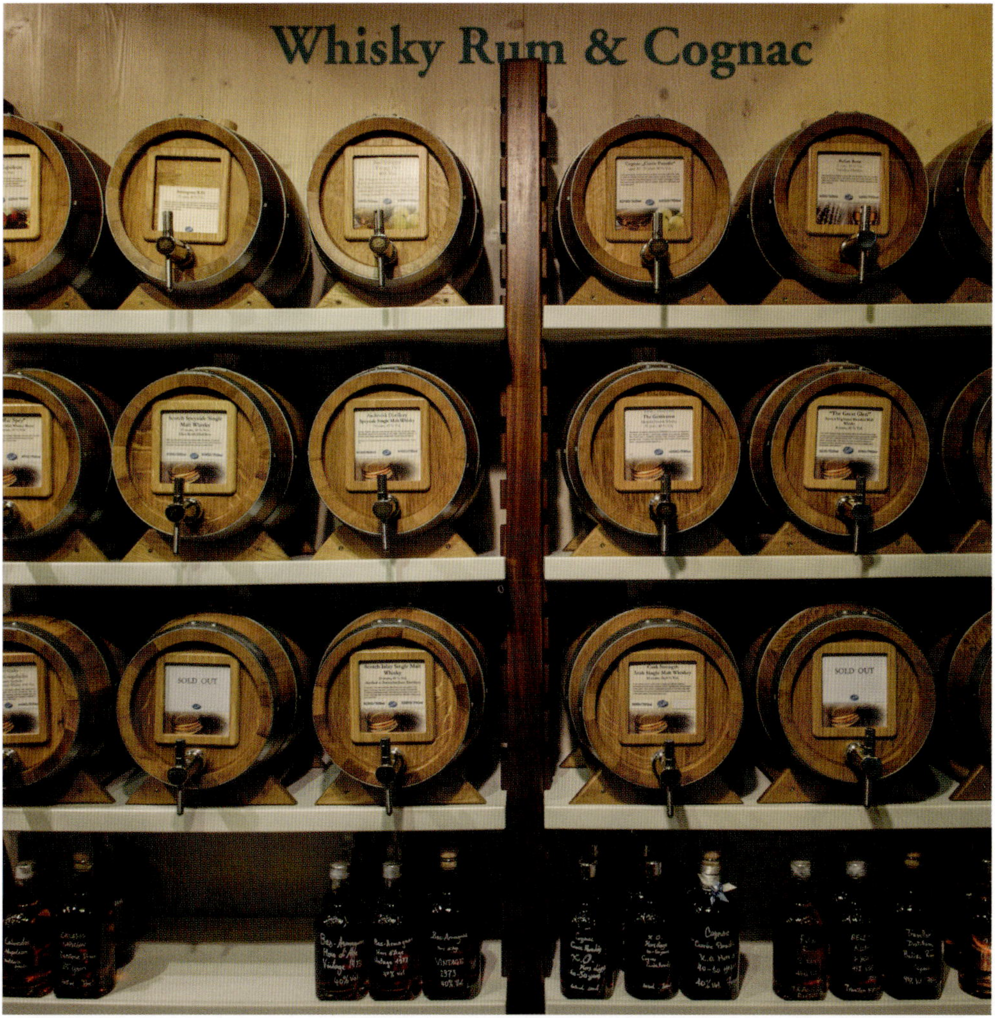
Whisky Rum & Cognac
SOLD OUT
SOLD OUT

FOOD

Area: CENTRAL
43 Wyndham Street

# TIVO WINE BAR

Wanna make friends with a young and lonely banker? You are in the top-manager lounge central, baby! This striking bar attracts the after-hours crowd from the nearby offices like a flame magnetically attracts butterflies. Success elusive? You'll be back for that generous happy hour with the complimentary delish snacks. Forget the bankers. Call for another round!

www.tivo.com.hk

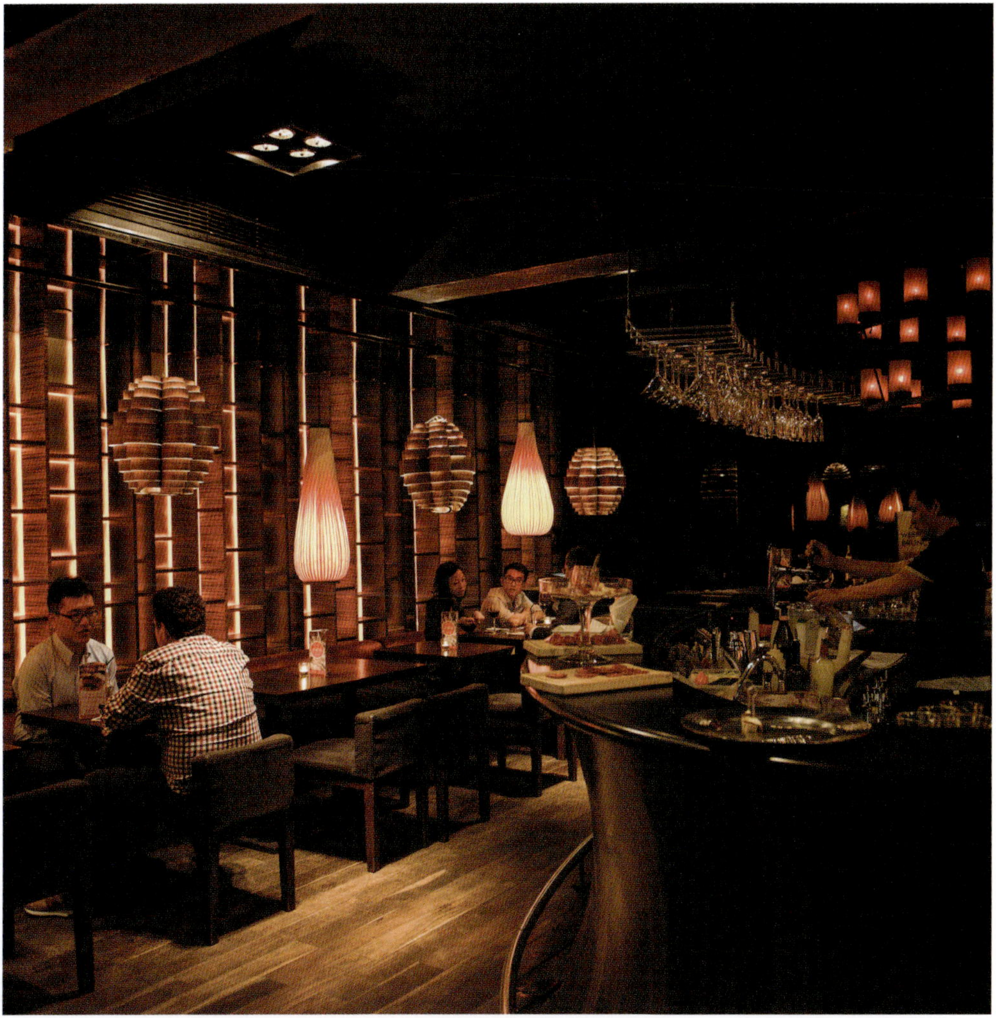

FOOD

Area: CENTRAL
1/F, 28 Elgin Street

# NAKED GURUME GYARARI

Soho's best hidden secret: a "gourmet gallery" (this is how the name translates) restaurant which is basically an experimental kitchen of two visionary chefs. You read the menu and get high in anticipation: it seems like all your favourite ingredients come together in one place! Fatty tuna belly, oysters, foie gras, lobster, jamon Iberico…rolled into "cake sushi", paired with guava gelato, sprinkled with crystalline ice leaves, whatever that means. Say what?! Stop. No more spoilers – come and experience it yourself.

www.naked.com.hk

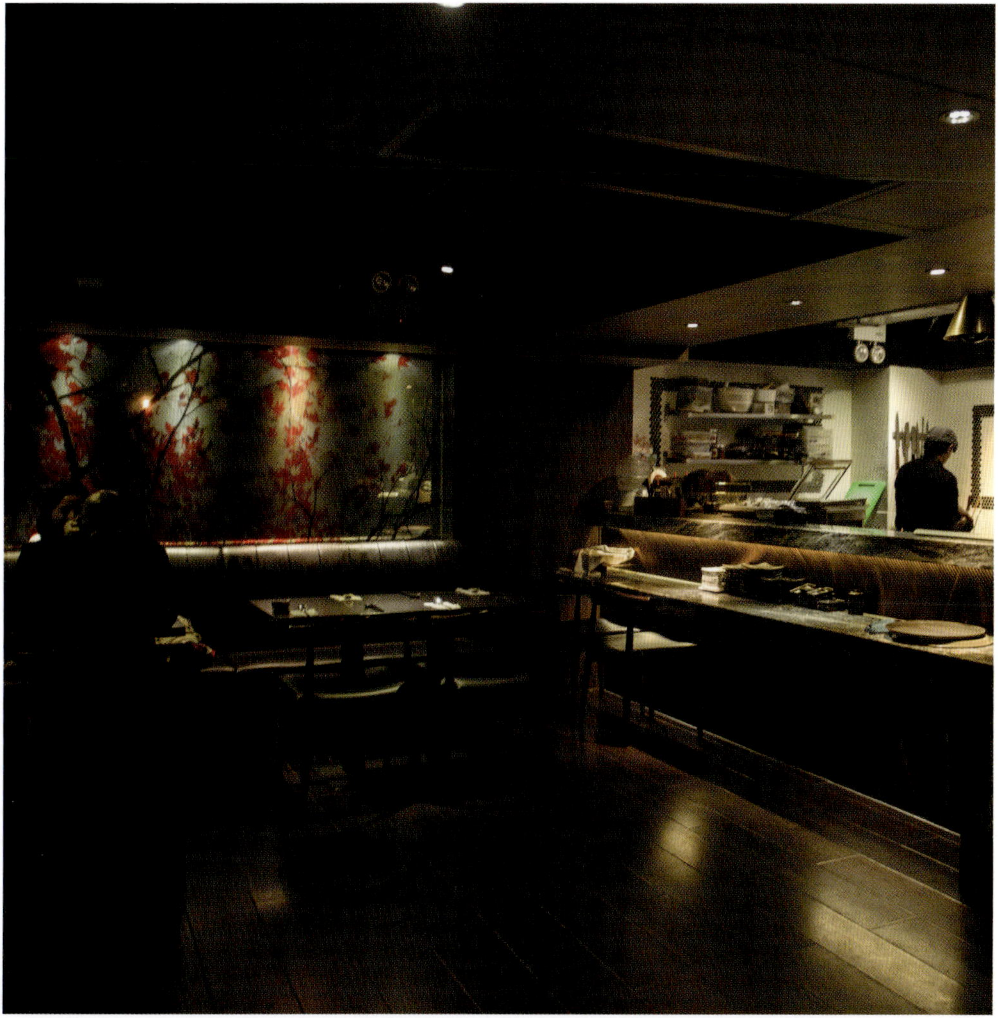

FOOD

Area: CENTRAL
61 Caine Road

# SEPA

Venetian bacaro, with Italy's youngest two Michelin-starred chef, Enrico Bartolini behind the captain's wheel. Home rolled pasta with melt-in-your-mouth beef cheek filling, mascarpone & truffle polenta soldiers, mixed seafood in the crispy batter, all washed down with that Venetian Martini…Small plates, massive delight.

www.sepa.com.hk

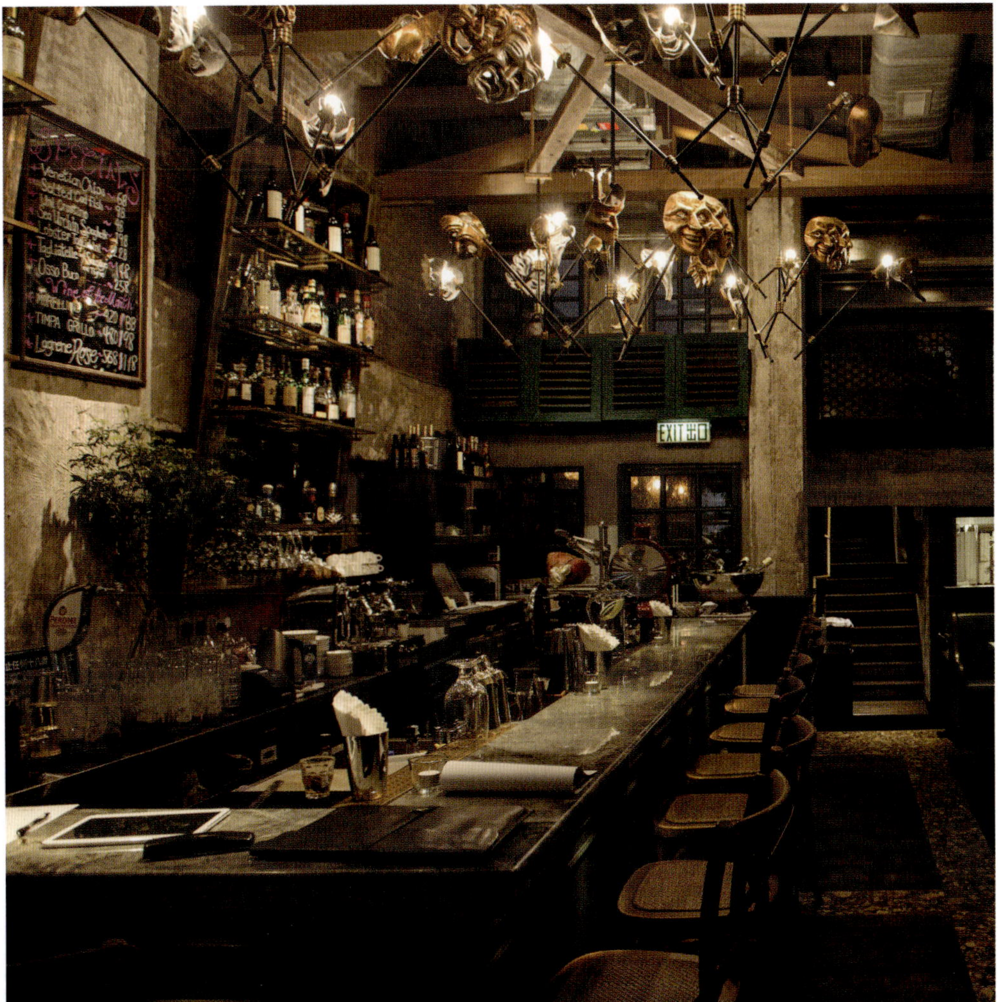
EXIT 出口

FOOD

Area: CENTRAL
PMQ, G/Floor JPC Building, 35 Aberdeen Street

# ABERDEEN STREET SOCIAL

The place to see and to be seen...eating. Splurge on dishes like Goat Cheese Churros with Truffle Honey or Smoked Eel & Cured Foie Gras at the most trending restaurant of the city and you can count yourself a true local foodie. Not cheap, but not shamelessly expensive for that class of dining experience. Epic Sunday brunch for those weekend feaster searchers.

www.aberdeenstreetsocial.hk

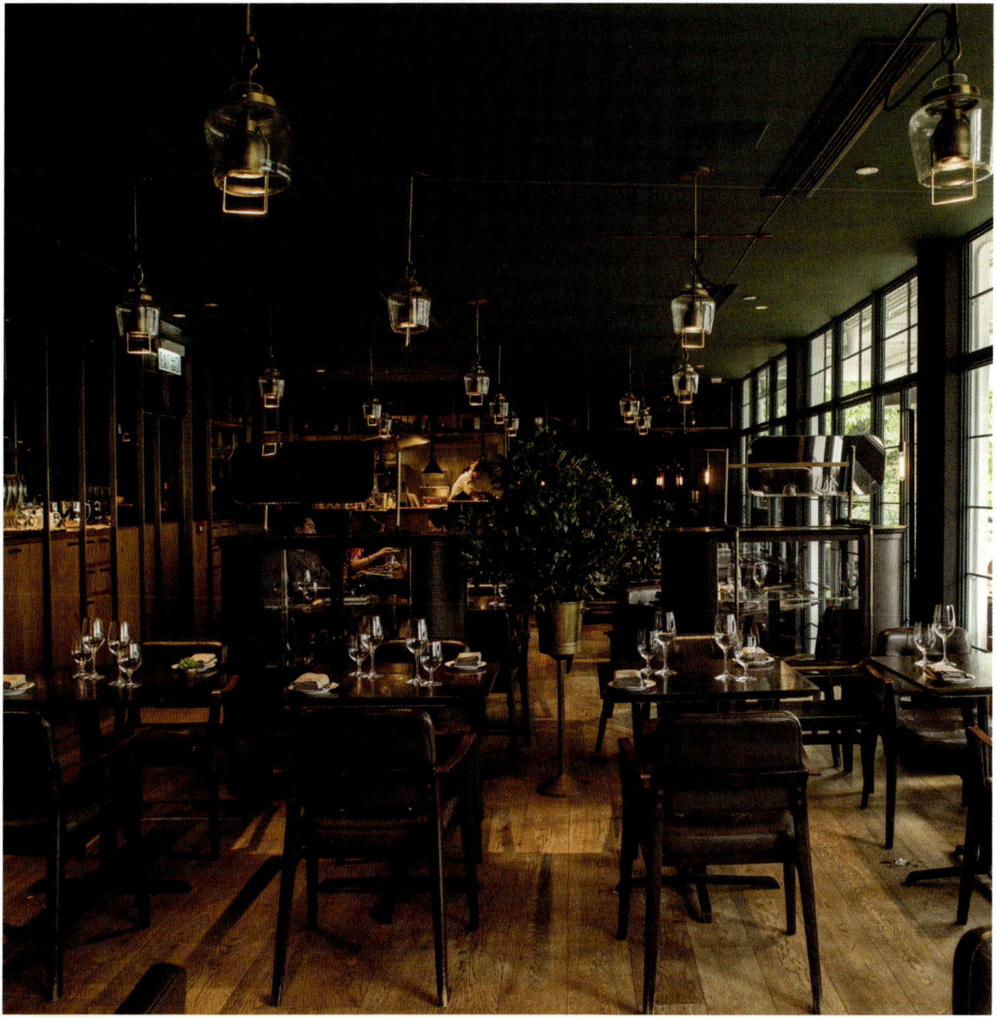

FOOD

Area: CENTRAL
G/F, 28 Elgin Street

# POSTO PUBBLICO

The rustic, authentic, hearty, generous, colourful food of Italian immigrants in New York…served in the heart of Hong Kong? Yes please. They don't call a city a melting pot for no reason!

www.postopubblico.com

HONG KONG'S
ORIGINAL
NEW YORK ITALIAN OSTE
* MAC & CHEESE $159
* FUSILLI W/ ROASTED CHERRY TOMATO, BREADED EGGPLANT HOMEMADE BOCCONCINI $169
* LINGUINI W/ SPICY PRAWN RAGU $169

FOOD

Area: CENTRAL
92 Wellington Street

# MANA!

Given that Hong Kong is a true foodie heaven, it's hard to be modest in your dining out: dim sums, fatty pork belly, greasy roasted duck, gourmet pizza, burgers of all sorts – everything in this city screams "Eat me!" One day you'll definitely feel like your belly needs some well-deserved rest. Which doesn't mean fasting at all – in Hong Kong even "clean eating" is gourmet! Mana! is the place where green is fun: this small chain of authentic eco-friendly deli is not only a healthy choice, but it's also addictively yum. All the outlets are extremely eco-conscious, too, with free water, energy-saving lights, water-saving toilets and paper straws and takeaway containers instead of nasty plastic stuff. Inspiring!

www.mana.hk

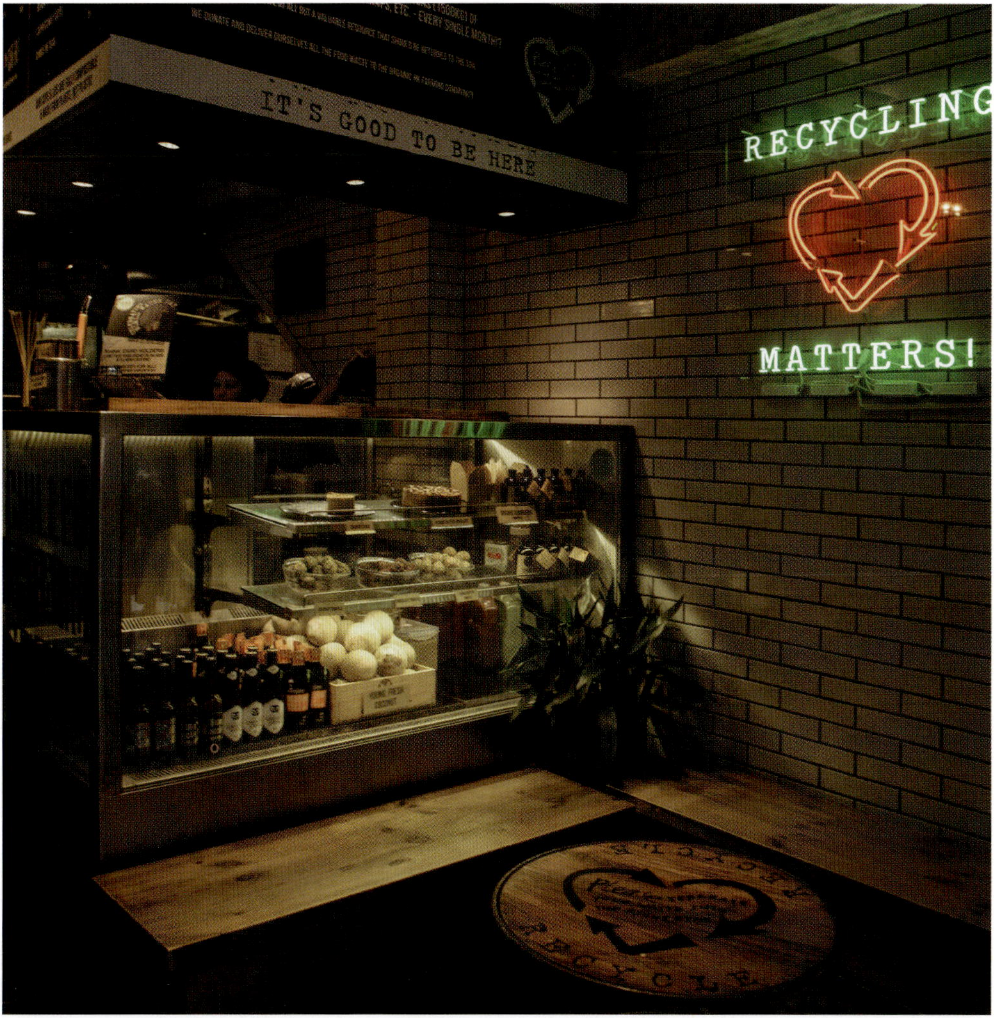
IT'S GOOD TO BE HERE
RECYCLING
MATTERS!
RECYCLE

FOOD

Area: CENTRAL
59 Caine Road

---

# THE MONOGAMOUS CHINESE

This is one of those precious secrets of the city. Just next to the Mid-Levels Escalators but hidden in a tiny side alley, The Monogamous is much loved by the expats and the travelling foodies. The dimly lit dining room looks like a movie set. The cuisine is excellent. If you are looking for an authentic and at the same time, unique experience, you will find it here.

---

www.themonogamouschinese.com

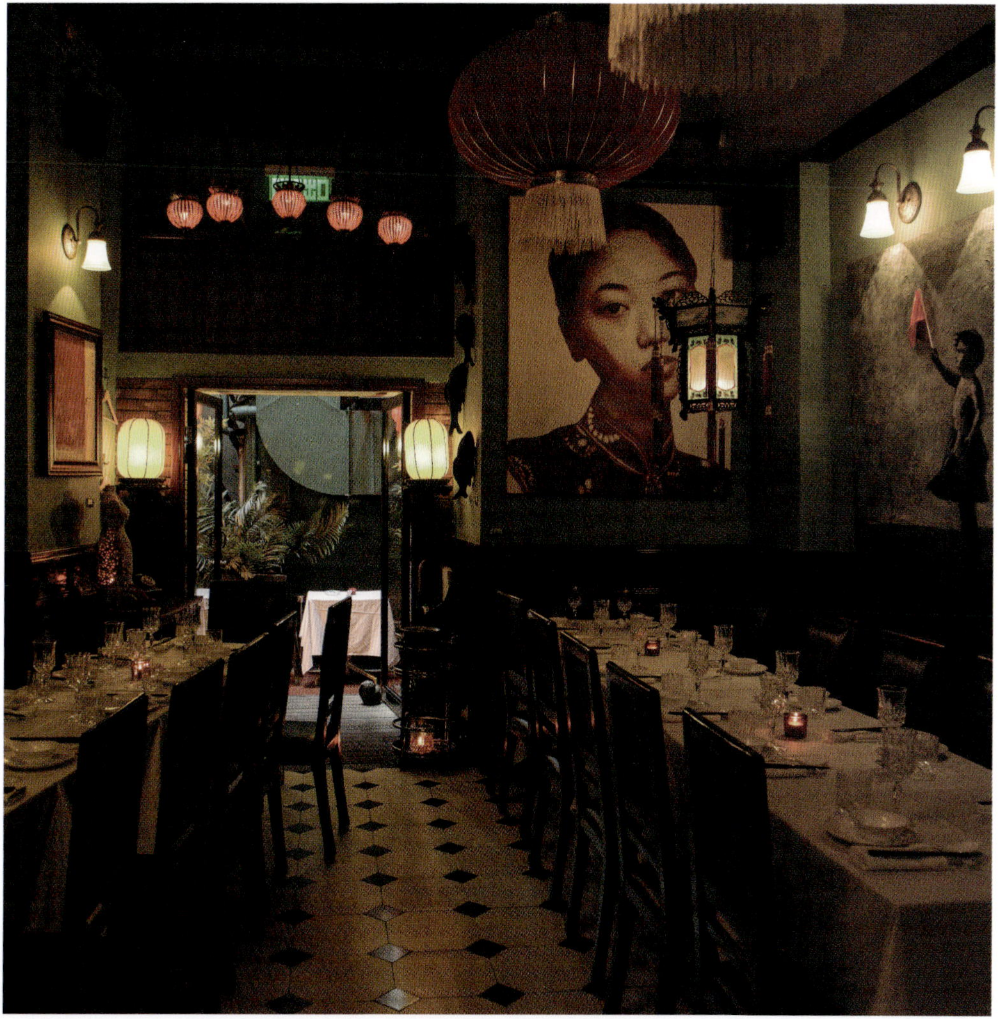

FOOD

Area: CENTRAL
17 Shelley street

# BUTCHERS BARREL

Meat lovers, look no further. The guys of Hong Kong's most favourite burger chain The Butcher's Club have opened a deli with dry-aged and grass-fed steaks, beef patties, farmers sausages, fresh bread and selection of lovely salads ready to go home with you. There is a nice choice of wine, too – so you don't have to worry. They've thoughtfully planned your perfect dinner in. The deli is sitting alongside the escalator, taking office workers up to their apartments – beyond smart!

www.thebutchers.club

FOOD TASTINGS
OUR SEAFOOD
IMPORTED
PREMIUM SUPPLIERS
LOSTE
BUTCHERS
B
BARREL

FOOD

Area: SHEUNG WAN
108 Hollywood Rd

# VASCO & ISONO

The finest of Spanish you can get out of Balearics: these two haute cuisine establishments, sharing the grounds of the PMQ complex, have a lot in common. Like, famed Spanish chef Paolo Casagrande of the two-Michelin-starred Restaurante Lasarte in Barcelona and that instant WOW factor that hits you as soon as the first dish is served. Si, senõr – this calls for a date!

www.vasco.com.hk | www.isono.com.hk

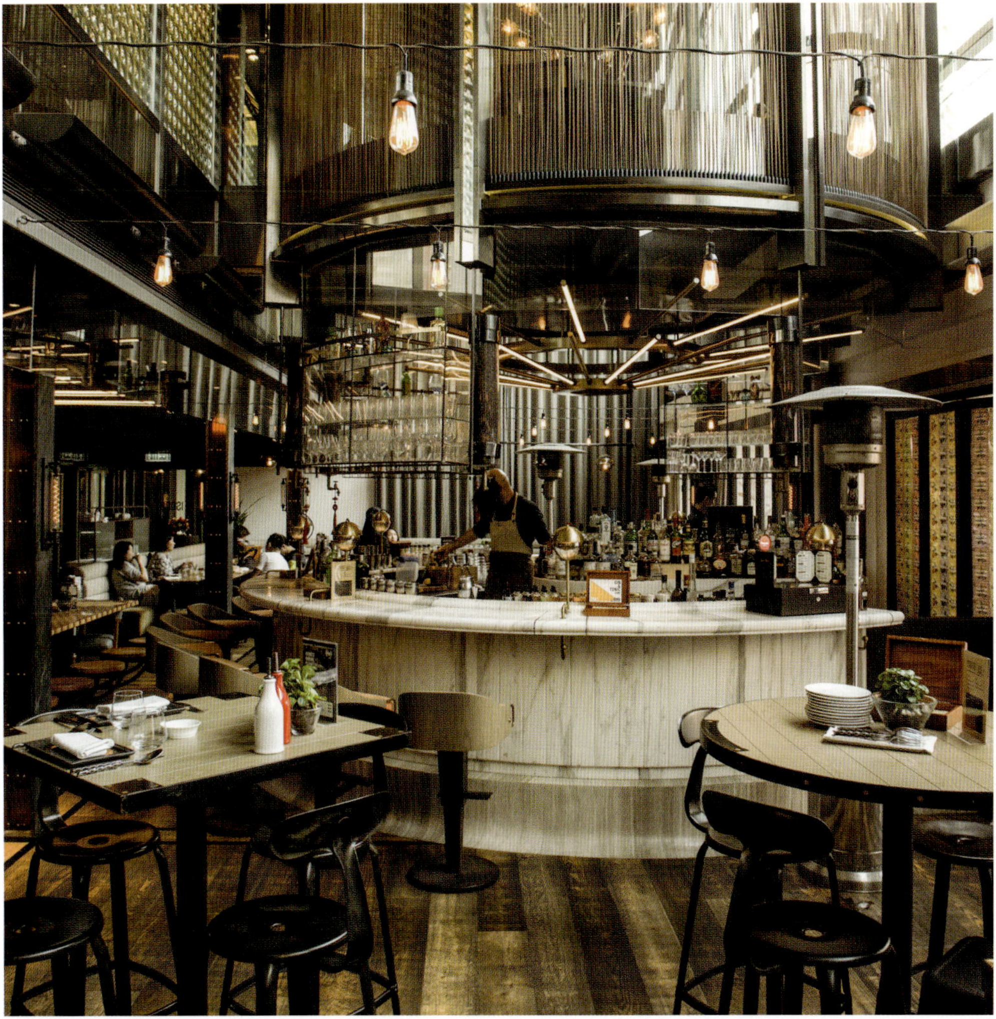

FOOD

Area: SHEUNG WAN
G/F, 163 Hollywood Road

# BIBO

Imagine dining in the semi-secret art gallery, packed with the private collection of the most curious art works. We are talking real Banksy, Daniel Arsham, Jeff Koons and Takashi Murakami here – all under one roof! Excuse us, but we'll go on with the name dropping: the mastermind behind the menu is the former chef of Alain Ducasse at the Plaza Athenee in Paris and L'Atelier de Joel Robuchon in London. Ok, enough now – this place is a stunner and a winner. Period. A must, even if you are up for just an aperitif.

www.bibo.hk

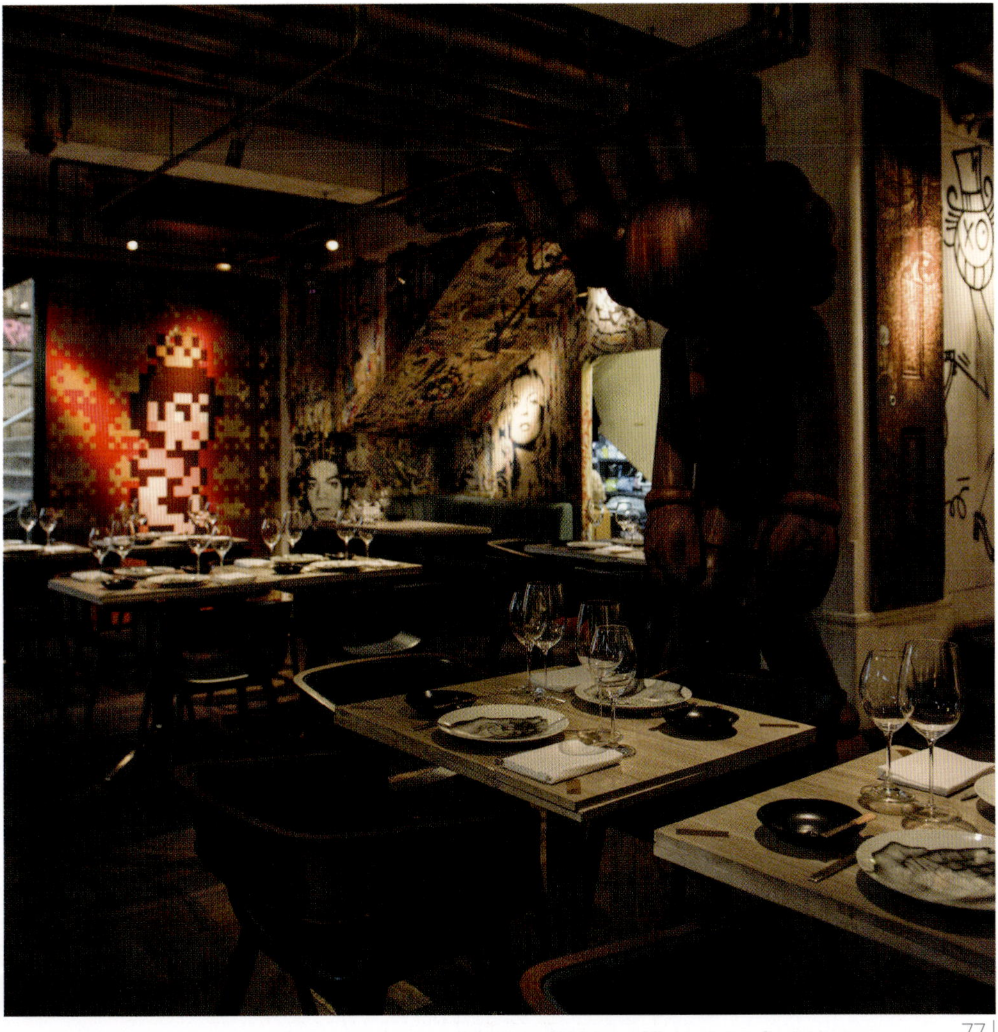

FOOD

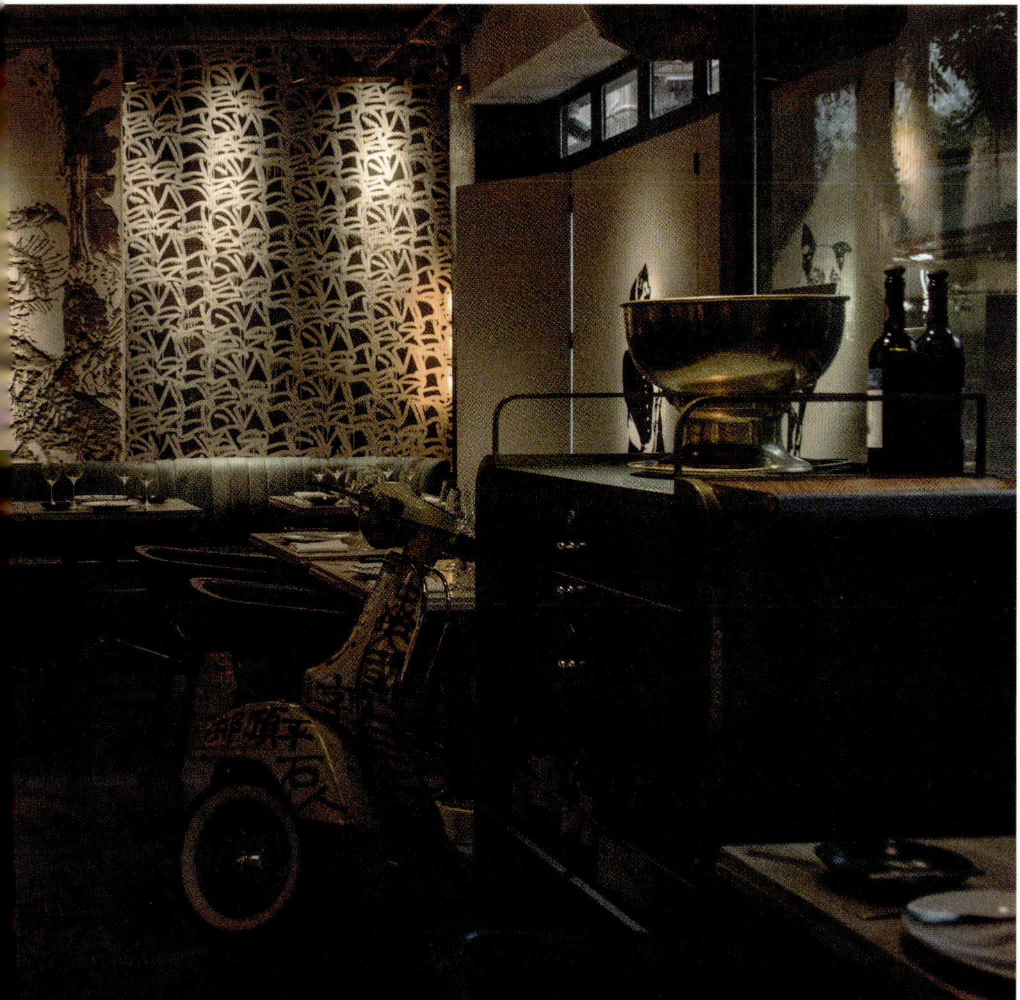

FOOD

Area: SHEUNG WAN
B 18 Tai Ping Shan Street

# TEAKHA

This itsy-bitsy tea room is just adorable. Get your chai and sit on the log (yes, a log!) outside or hide in the cosy café on a rainy day. Treat yourself with a home baked cake. Make friends with a tea maker and try bribing her to make you a cup of Earl Grey (spoiler: you'll fail as they sell only unusual teas here). A perfect spot to rest your legs while exploring the über-hip neighbourhood of Tai Ping!

www.teakha.com

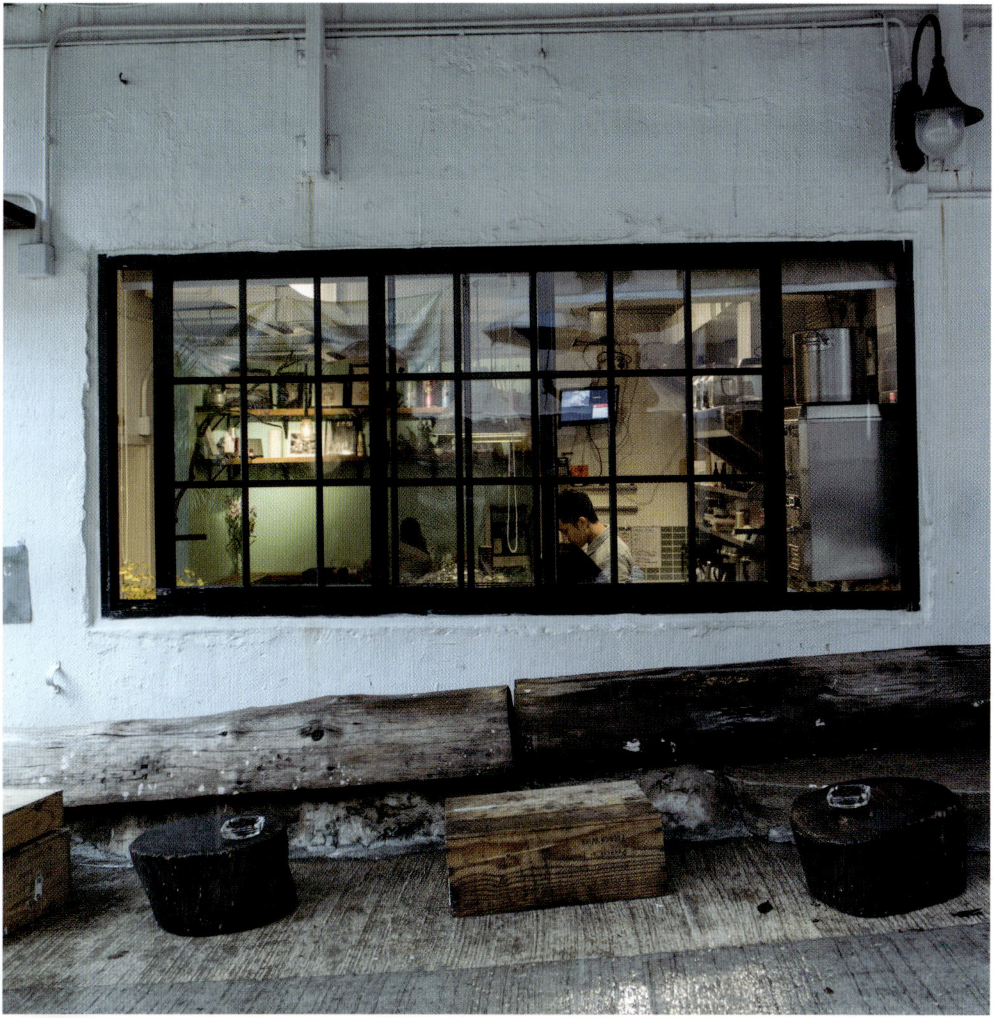

## FOOD

Area: WAN CHAI
62 Johnston Road

# THE PAWN

A multi-level dining institution set up in a legendary 3-storey building that used to be a city's famous pawnshop. Not hungry yet? Put your killer stiletto and backless dress on and march to the bar – you really can't say you've seen Hong Kong's social life without checking this legend out.

www.thepawn.com.hk

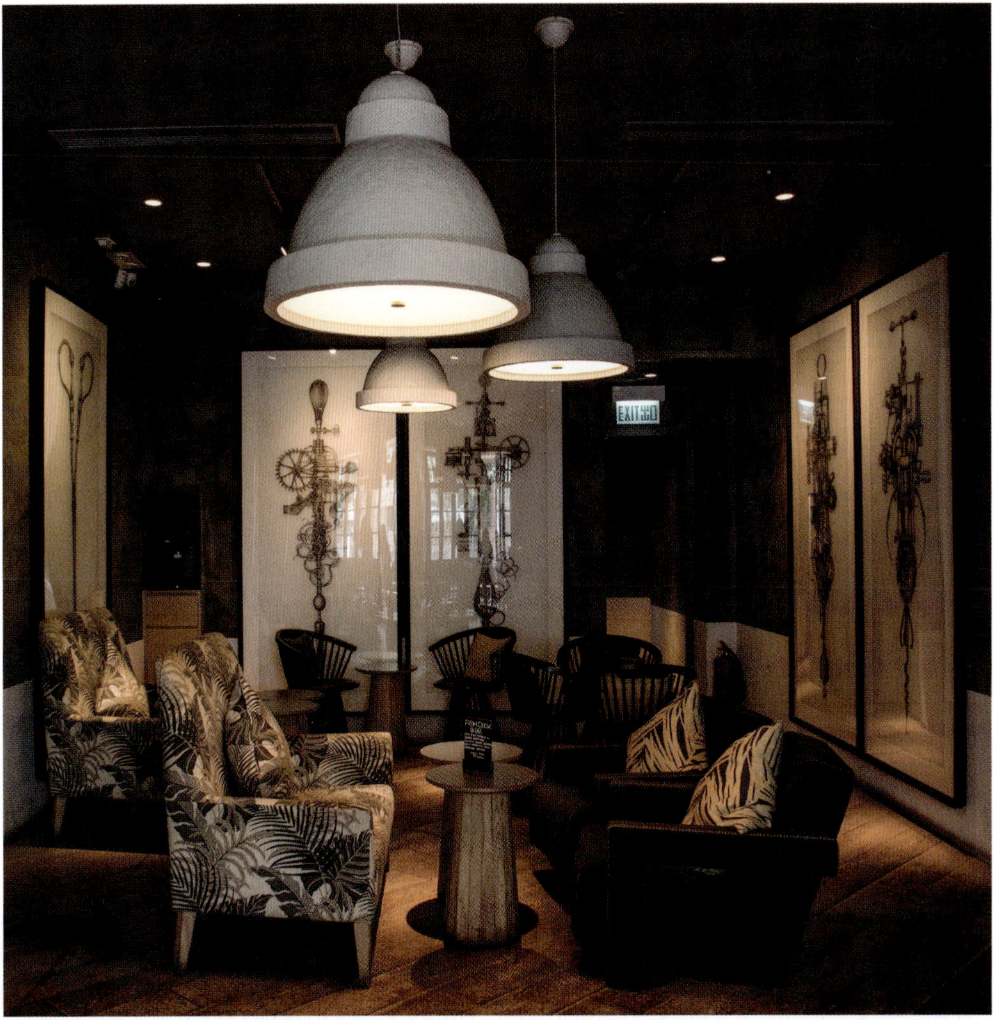
EXIT

FOOD

Area: WAN CHAI
1-7 Ship St

# HAM & SHERRY

It was blue&white vintage looking tiles that caught our eye, but then it was the Spanish cold cuts and tapas that stole our hearts! And then we almost left our liver at the venue's "secret" Back Bar – end of story. A happy end though!

www.hamandsherry.hk

SPECIALS:
TUNA TARTAR
PAN CON
ANCHOVY
TUNA piquillo pepper
GARLIC FRIES
SQUID
TUNA TARTAR
TUNA PIQUILLO
PANCON. ANCHOVY

FOOD

Area: WAN CHAI
22 Ship Street

# 22 SHIPS

Some name-dropping won't hurt in 22 Ships' case: this hip cafe is a baby of British celebrity chef Jason Atherton, who's a protégé of Ferran Adrià. Now forget what you've just heard, as this venue is as laid-back and casual as a simple Spanish tavern. It's tiny and unpretentious, with an open layout and cheerful waiters. Grab a seat at the "window bar", order a glass of light jerez and get ready for the fork fight over the tapas plates full of seafood paella, grilled octopus, goats curd with Iberico ham and other delights. Sharing is not always easy, you know.

www.22ships.hk

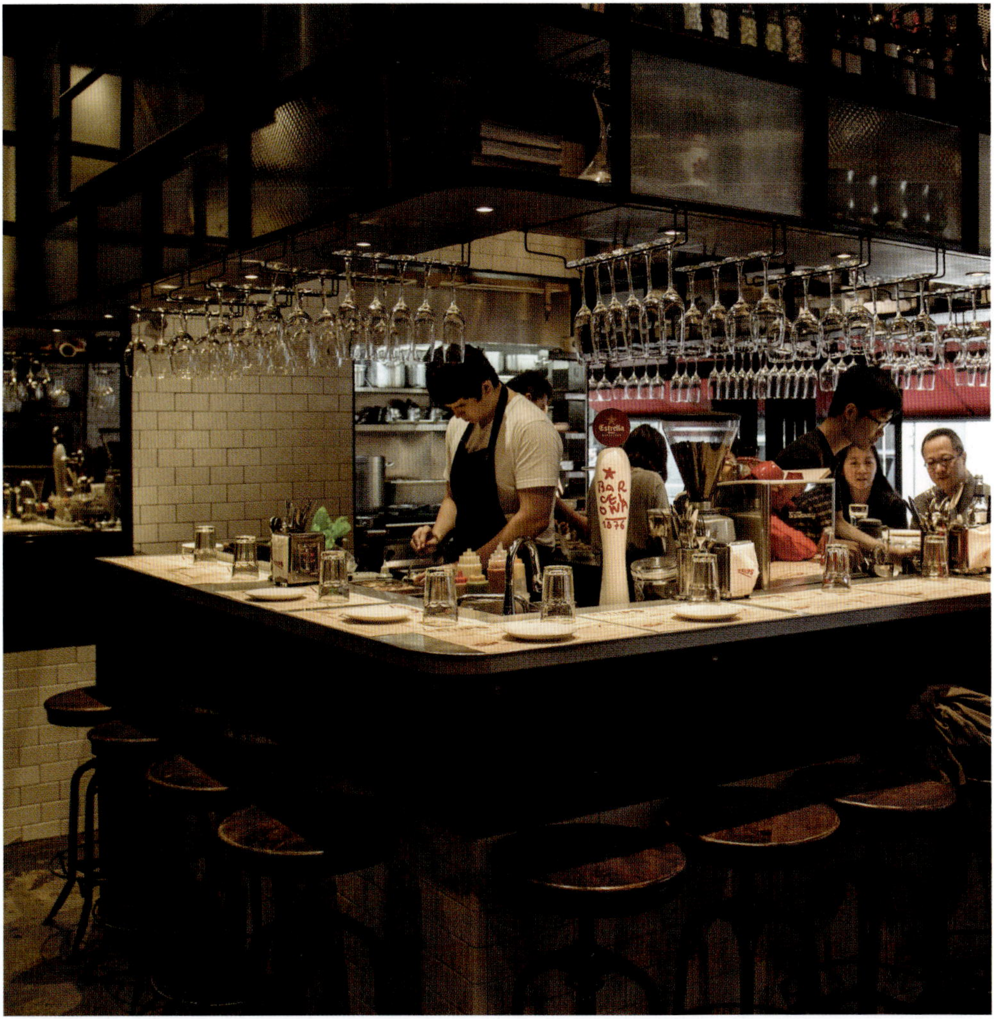
Estrella
1876

FOOD

Area: REPULSE BAY
G/F, Shop 114-115, The pulse Repulse Bay, 28 Beach Rd

# HOTSHOT

California dreamin': come sit under the vintage surf boards, sip on your classic Americana-style thick milkshake, and hang out with a gigantic Bart Simpson. Repulse Bay has never been cooler!

www.hotshot.hk

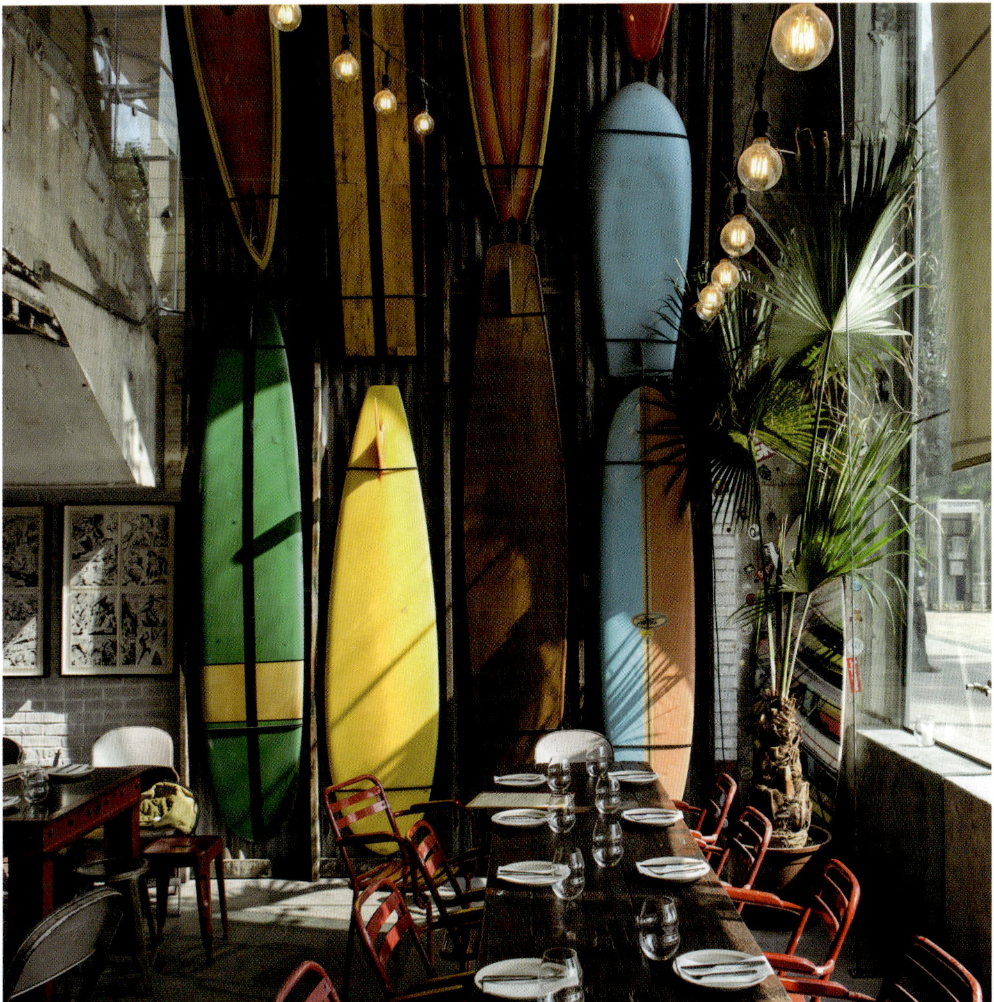

FOOD

Area: TSIM SHA TSUI
29+30F, 1 Peking Road

# AQUA

Lucy in the sky, with diamonds. Blow dust off your jewels, this gem in the clouds is worth it. This spacious top floor venue has this "sexy cool" vibe that makes your heart skip a beat when you arrive: those gigantic windows overlooking the neversleeping city, the ships passing by underneath, the beaming lights of skyscrapers…It's all about the view! Get yourself a glass of prosecco to get started – you do need some bubbles to put that vertigo on a leash.

www.aqua.com.hk

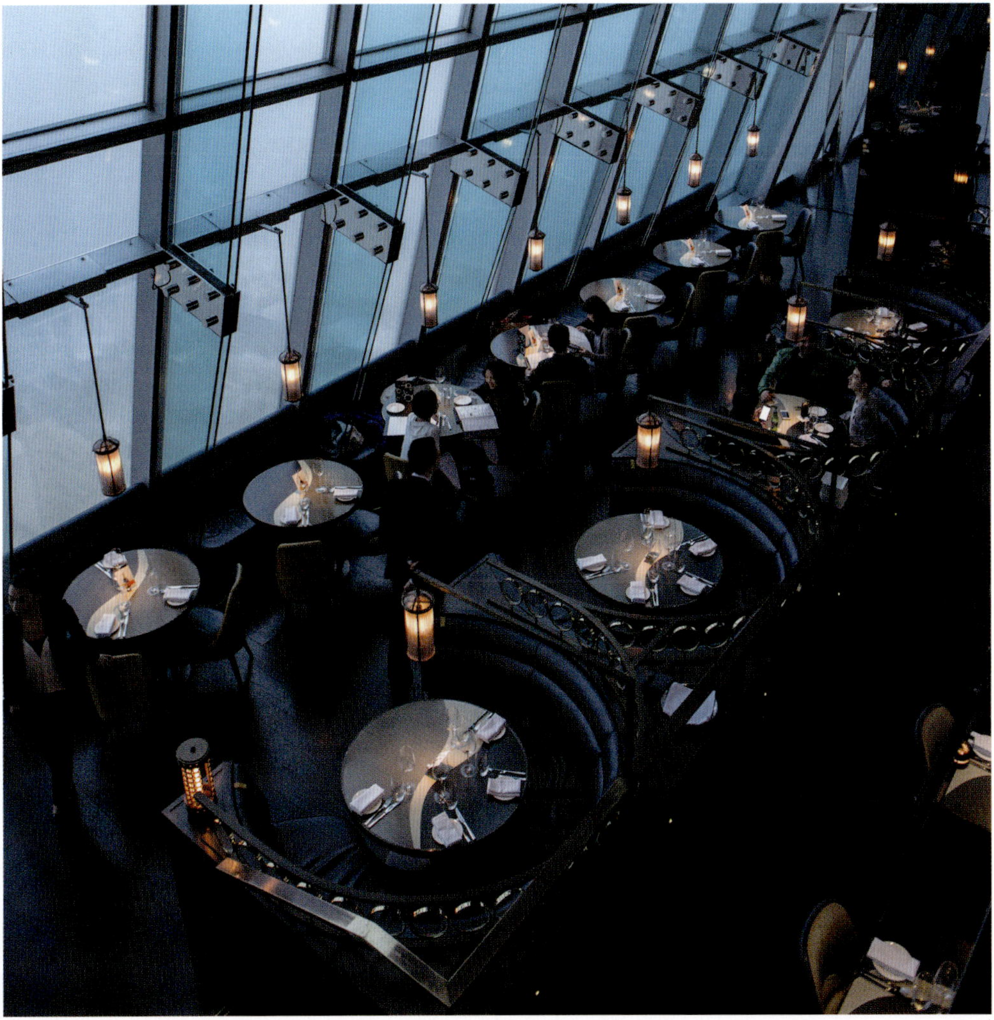

FOOD

Area: TSIM SHA TSUI
28/F, 1 Peking

# HUTONG

Come around sunset time, get to the 28th floor of the business centre in the chaotic Kowloon side of the city. Step out of the elevator and freeze in awe: this place is genuinely spectacular. Its dark, mysterious ambiance is cheered up by the traditional red lanterns and the wishing tree's scarlet ribbons floating in the air. A fairy tale Old China play pretend, with the modern day Hong Kong skyline under your feet.

www.hutong.com.hk/experience

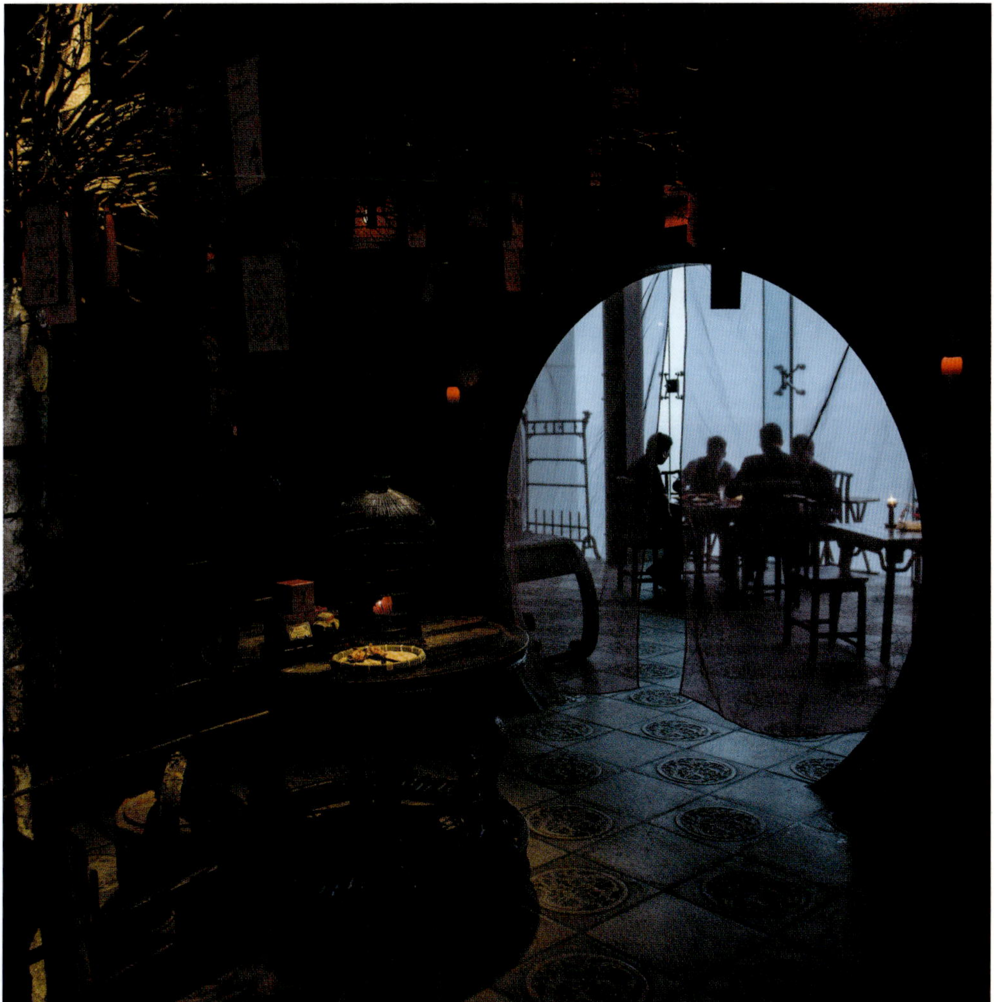

FOOD

Area: TSIM SHA TSUI
Level 21, The One, 100 Nathan Road

# WOOLOOMOOLOO PRIME

If you really need a reason to leave the HK Island and spend a night at the Kowloon side, this posh rooftop Australian steakhouse might be the best reason to do so. The open air bar terrace has some of the best views in the city.

www.wooloo-mooloo.com

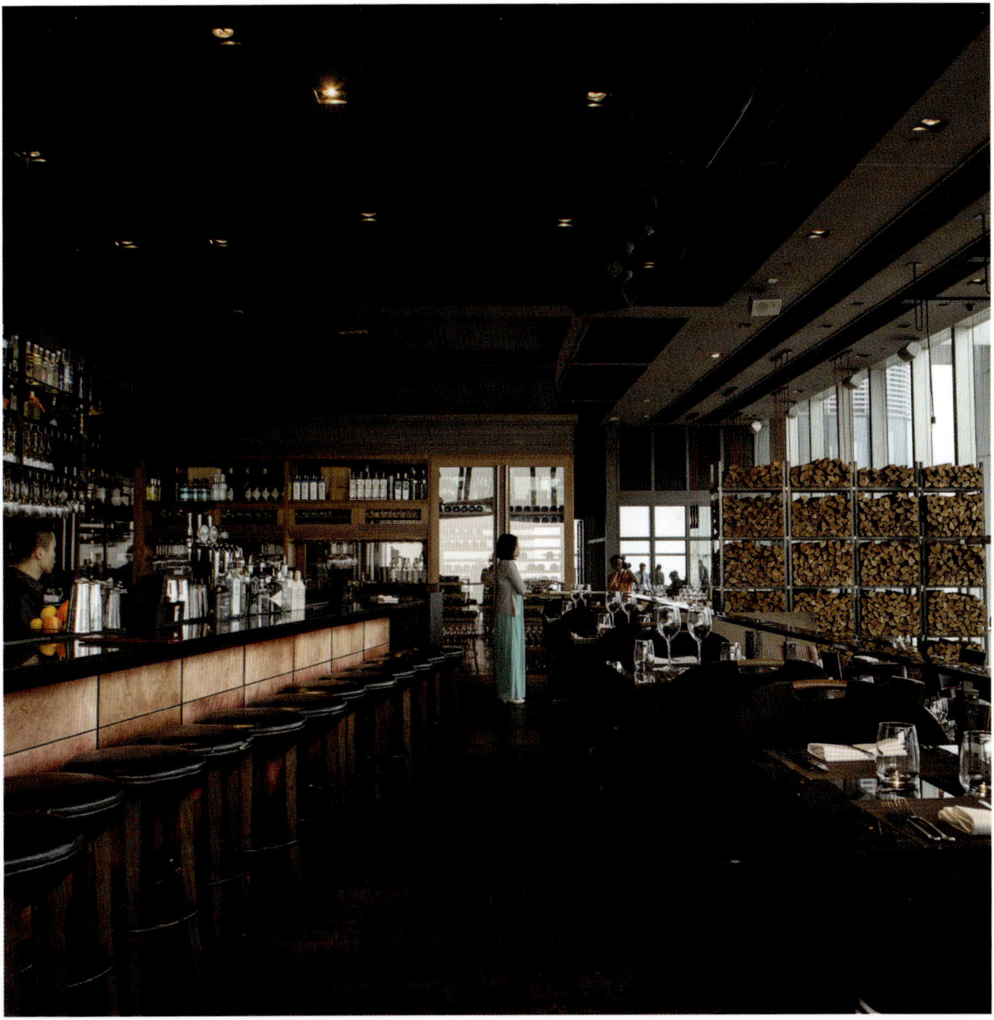

FOOD

Area: TSIM SHA TSUI
17 Science Museum Rd

# ABOVE & BEYOND
## at Hotel Icon

The classy set up, the classic view – on lagoon, cruise ships passing by and naked rooftops of Tsim Sha Tsui. And the classic menu to match: welcome to the Cantonese cuisine heaven. You really don't need to sit under the red, paper lantern for an authentic experience – interior by Terence Conran and a little black dress does the trick, just as good if the chef behind your back knows his business well. Don't be shy and go extravagantly intemperate with your order: go for baked wague beef buns, dim sums with sea urchin, steamed coral crab, honey-glazed bbq pork… doesn't matter how full you are, there will not be a single crumb left!

www.hotel-icon.com

97

FOOD

Area: STANLEY
88 Stanley Main St

# THE BOATHOUSE

A staple for a sunny Sunday: morning walk at Stanley beach promenade followed by a lunch of seafood platter and crispy Chardonnay at The Boathouse – legendary, but yet 100% laidback. You can't miss this cute yellow mansion on the corner!

www.cafedecogroup.com

99

ART

We won't discover America by stating this: Hong Kong is South East Asia's biggest art hub. The most massive fair, Art Basel Hong Kong, is an annual creative Sabbath, laced with a few side-fests and dozens of fringe events and happenings. This is definitely a fun thing to do, soaking in the visual content, watching creative minds from all around the globe, mingling with the artsy community and maybe even witnessing some big deals being closed right there, in the middle of this madhouse. Art weeks aside, this city breathes art: every second door of any cool hood is a gallery, where any curious "passer-buy" – not to mention a serious connoisseur – is very welcome.

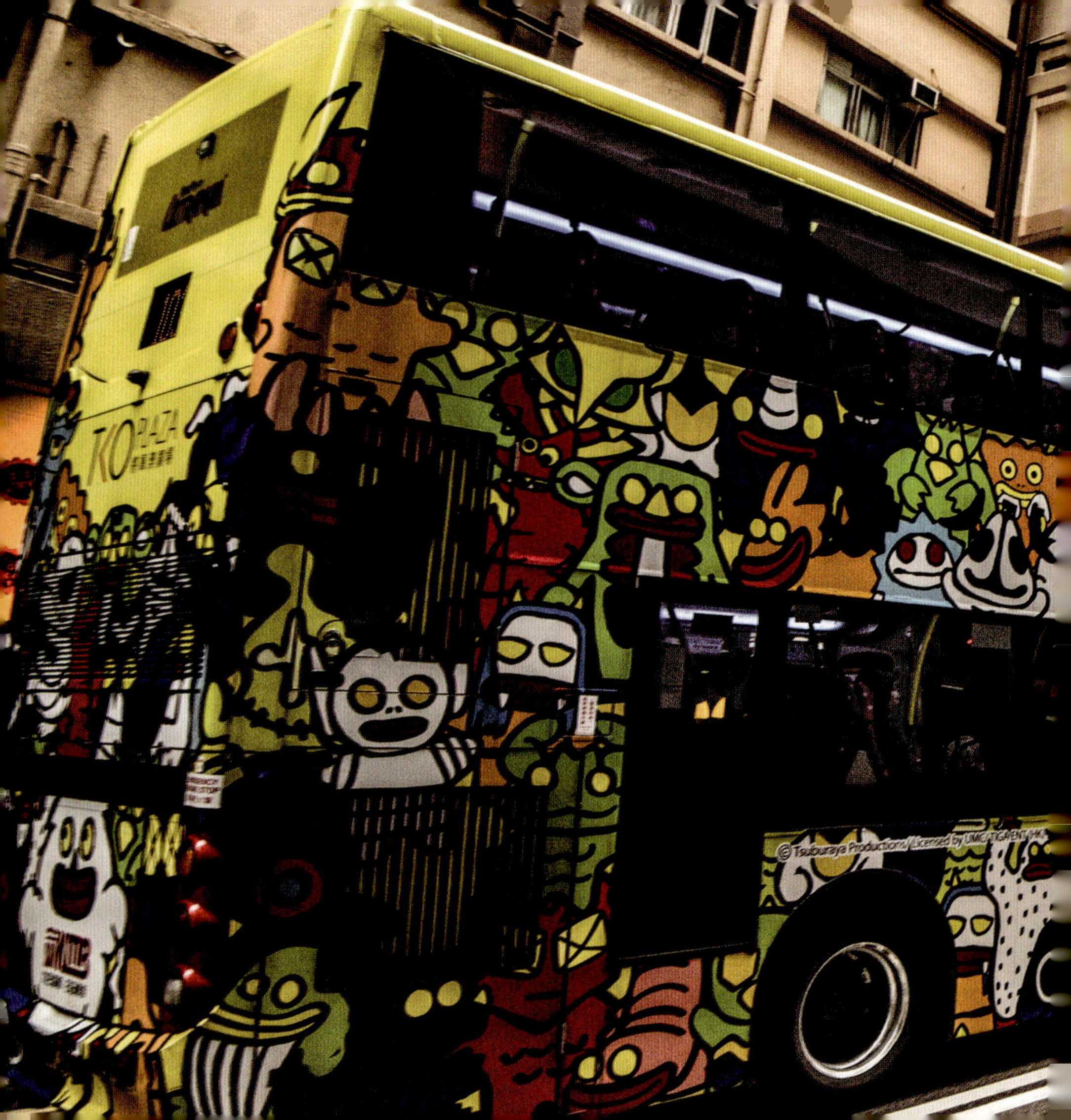
KO PLAZA
© Tsuburaya Productions/Licensed by UMG

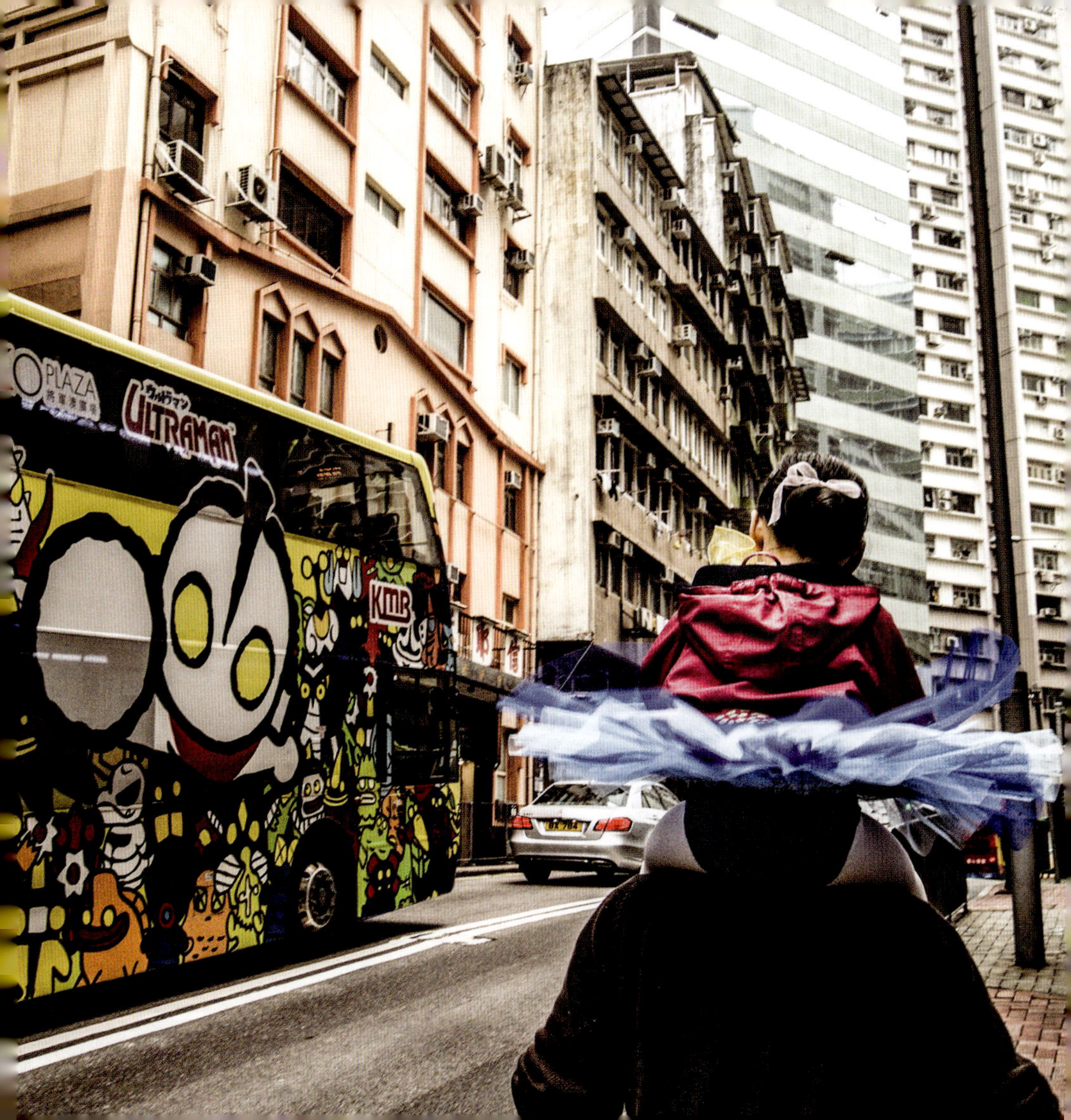
PLAZA
ULTRAMAN
KMB

ART

Area: CENTRAL
74 Hollywood road

# LA GALERIE

The finest selection of the photography brought to Hong Kong by the French couple of art connossieurs. From reportage to the fantasy visionary creations, from b&w to neon hues, from the world famous names to upcoming young artists – there is never a dull moment in here.

www.lagalerie.hk

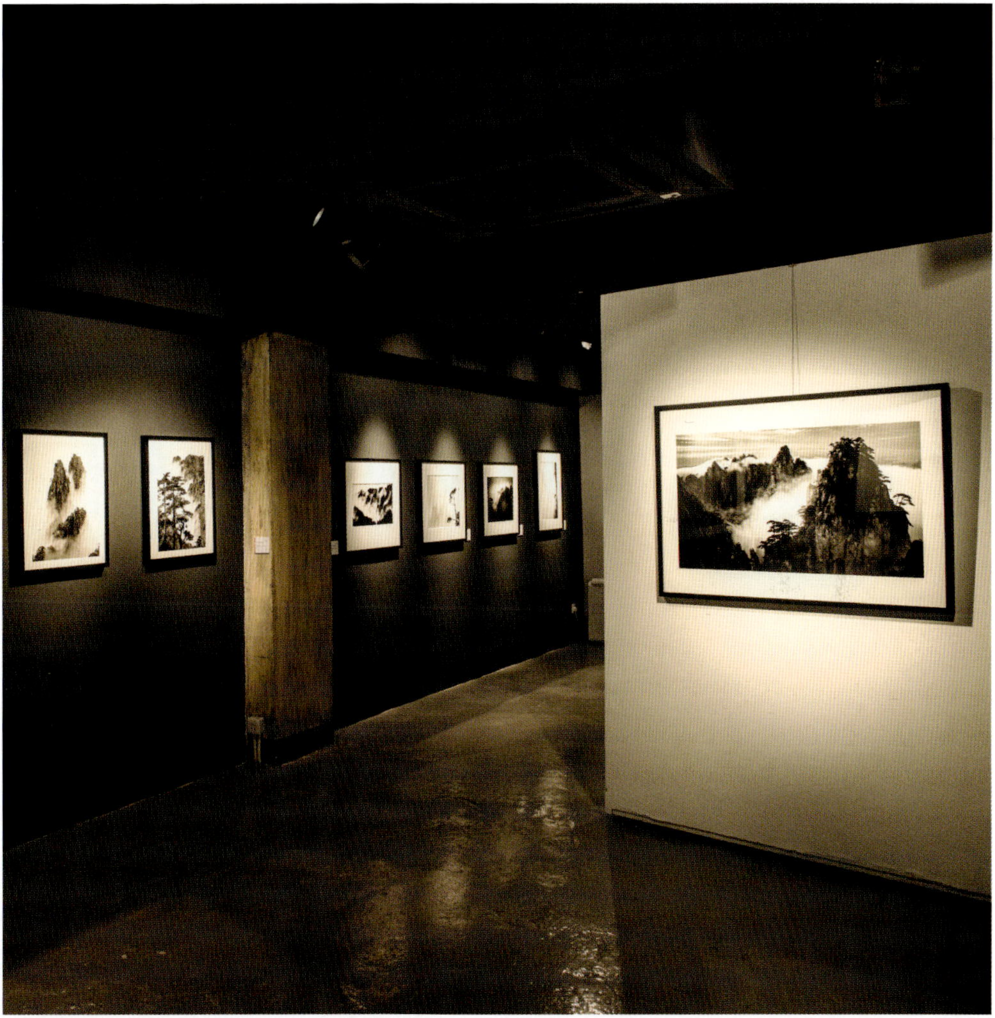

ART

Area: CENTRAL
G/F - 3/F, W Place, 52 Wyndham Street

# OPERA GALLERY

Big names: from Chagall and Magritte to Hurst and Murakami. Impressive geography – outlets in eleven countries around the globe. With the Hong Kong gallery, you get impressed even before you enter the building – the multi-level building with the large windows displaying the most catchy artworks, magnify for any art lover, be it a PRO or an amateur. Get ready to meet some of the old favourites and get closer to the new trends in the contemporary art movement. This art mogul has something for everyone, so step in and let the art rule your world for a bit.

www.operagallery.com

SUH
JEONG
MIN
INSIDE THE BARK
OF THE MULBERRY
TREE
22 MARCH – 6 APRIL 2016
OPERA GALLERY
OPERA GALLERY
THE CENTRIUM

ART

Area: CENTRAL
118 Hollywood Road

# AGNES B'S
## Librairie Gallery

The wonder woman of French fashion might have dressed legends from David Bowie to Tom Yorke, but these days Agnès b. is all about visual arts – from film directing to the supporting of street artists. Although the designer has 128 stores around the world, Librarie Galerie is her only art space outside of Paris. It is always bursting with some curious activities – look in and discover what's this month's buzz is about.

asia.agnesb.com/en/bside

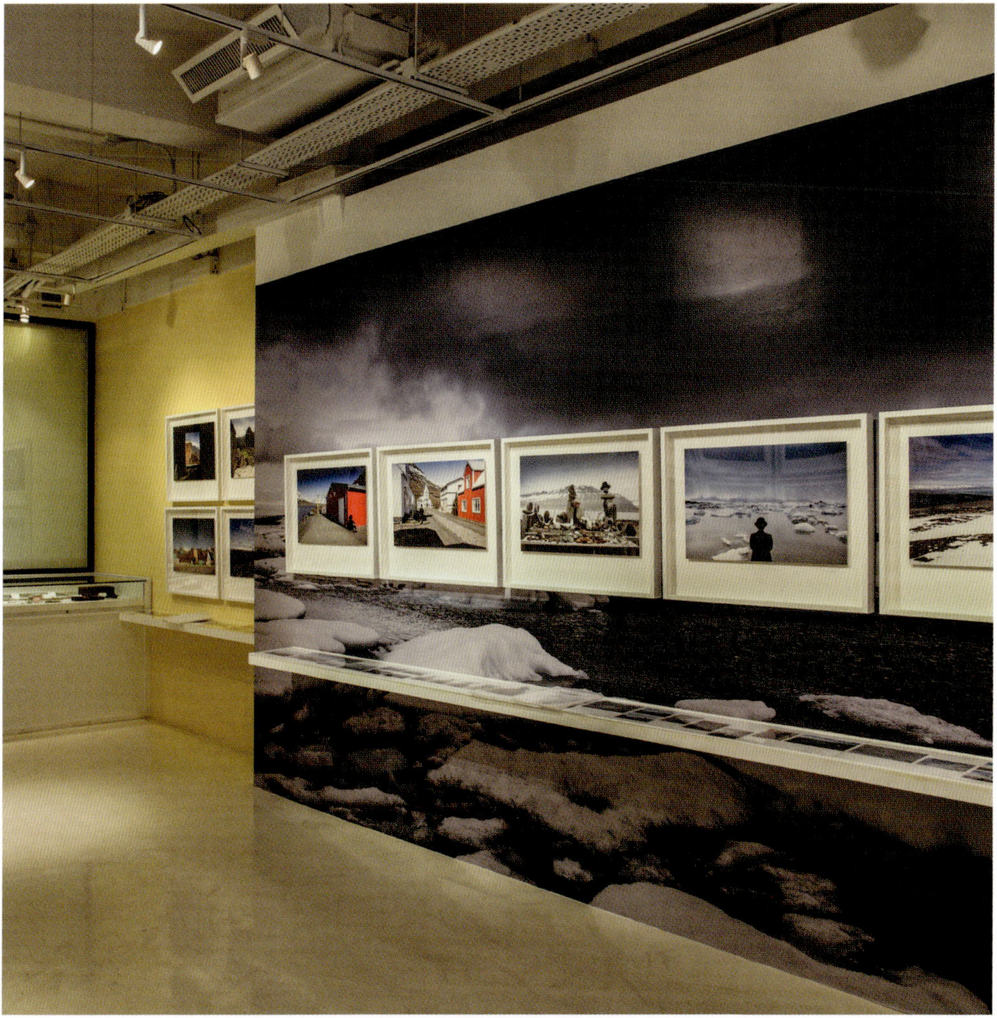

ART

Area: CENTRAL
G/F 129 - 133 Wellington Street

# ART BEATUS

Chinese contemporary art has been a massive hit for the past decade and it's still going strong. It's fresh, and it sells like Michelin-starred dim sums. No wonder it is Art Beatus' main focus! Pop in this clever gallery to see what's hot in the art world today.

www.artbeatus.com

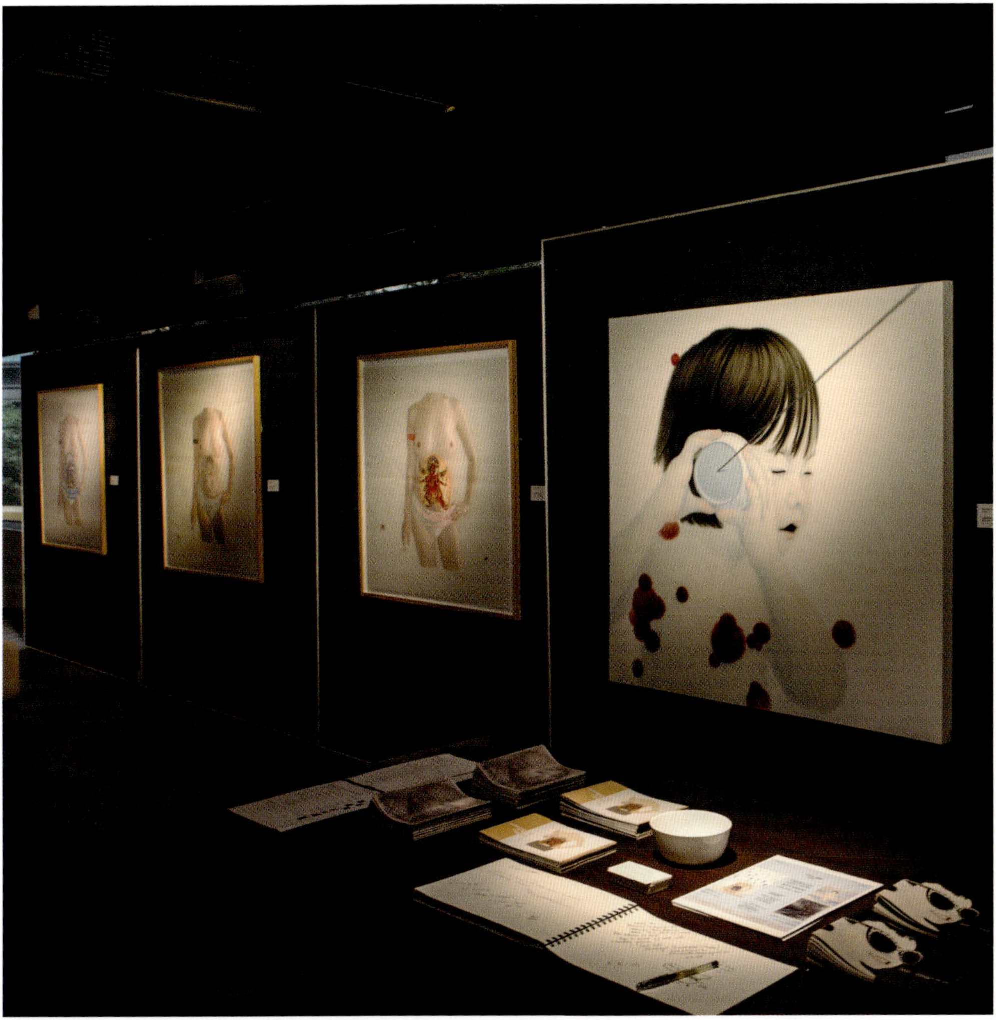

Area: CENTRAL
LG/F, Ezra Lane, Lower Hollywood Road

# GECKO LOUNGE

Intimate bar tucked away in the backstreet under the escalator – with all those details given, it's actually fancier than it sounds! The cocktails are fab (don't miss that mean margarita!) but you are here because of music. Live jazz sessions every Tuesday and Thursday – sing along and send the notes with requests. They are very welcome.

www.facebook.com/Geckoclubhk

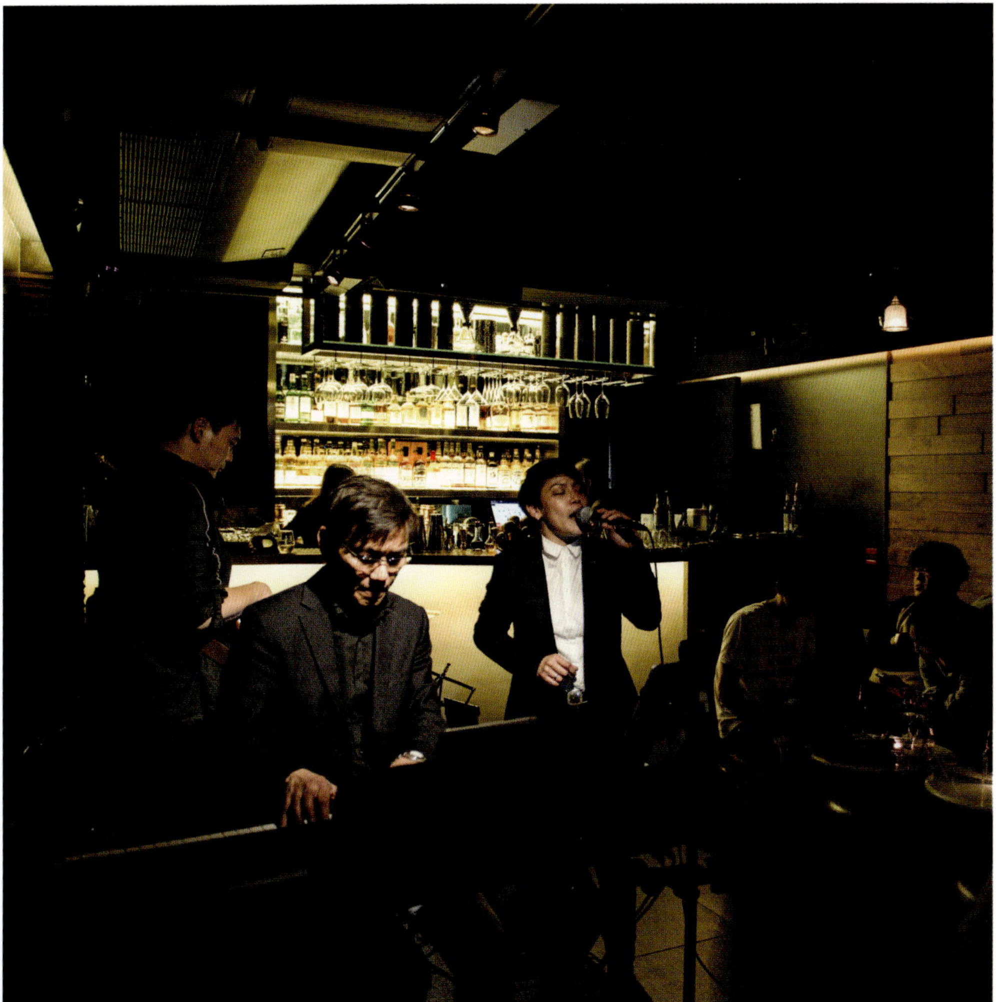

ART

Area: CENTRAL
52 and 54 Sai Street

# SIN SIN FINE ART

The best of Chinese and South Eastern Asia artists in the hip neighborhood of PoHo. Keep your eyes open: there is always something interesting cooking up in this space. Double luck if you happen to bump into the flamboyant owner and the sole curator of the art space, Ms Sing Sing Man herself – she's quite a character!

www.sinsinfineart.com

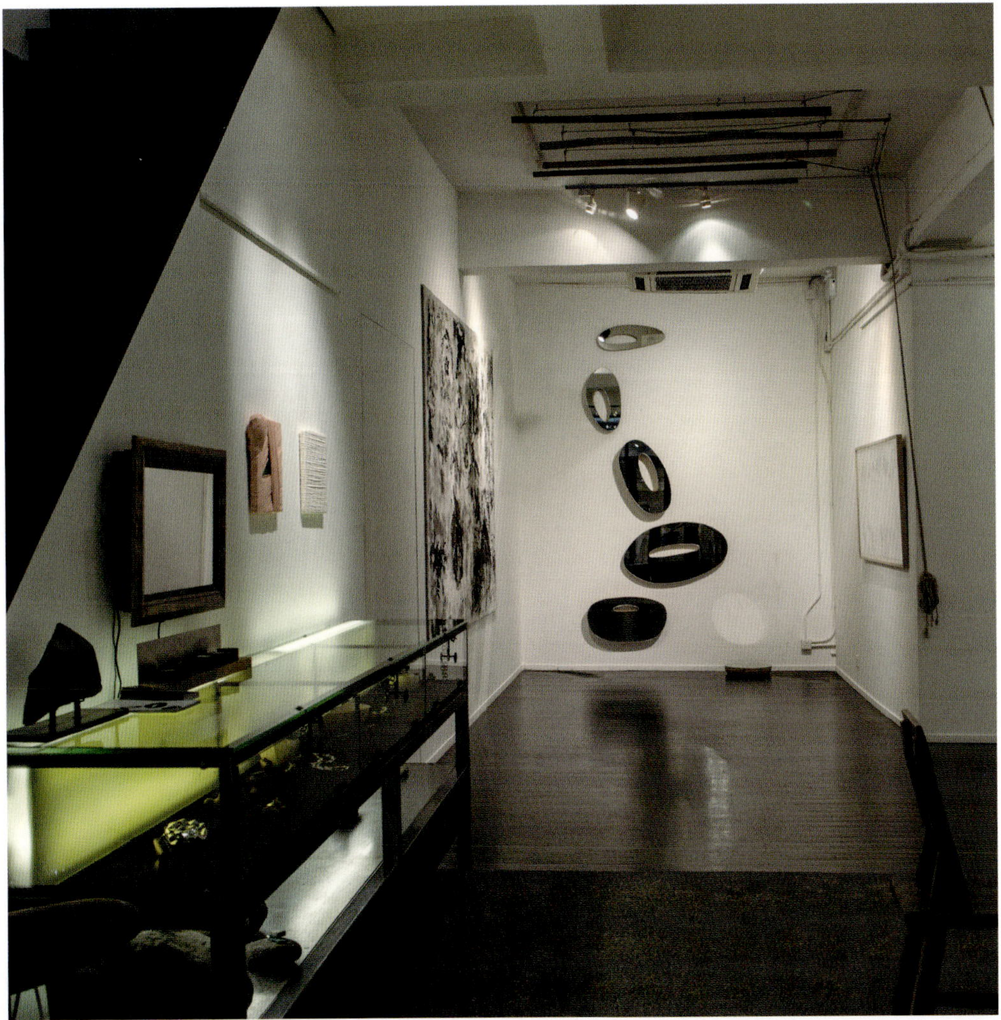

FASHION

Packing for your Hong Kong trip? Take bare essentials only, because after just a few days in this city your luggage will be blown up with all the new exciting outfits you won't be able to pass up on! The HK is agent provocateur, shopping-wise: it influences and ultimately seduces you, with what the bar crowd looks like, what a cool cat barista in your favourite coffee shop wears…and you just want it all. Badly!

However, the shopping experience in Hong Kong is not only about fashion. Surely, you'll stuff your luggage with some vintage dresses, new promising Asian brands and some crazy shoes to blend in with the city's hipster community? But watch out, there is way more to spend your cash on!

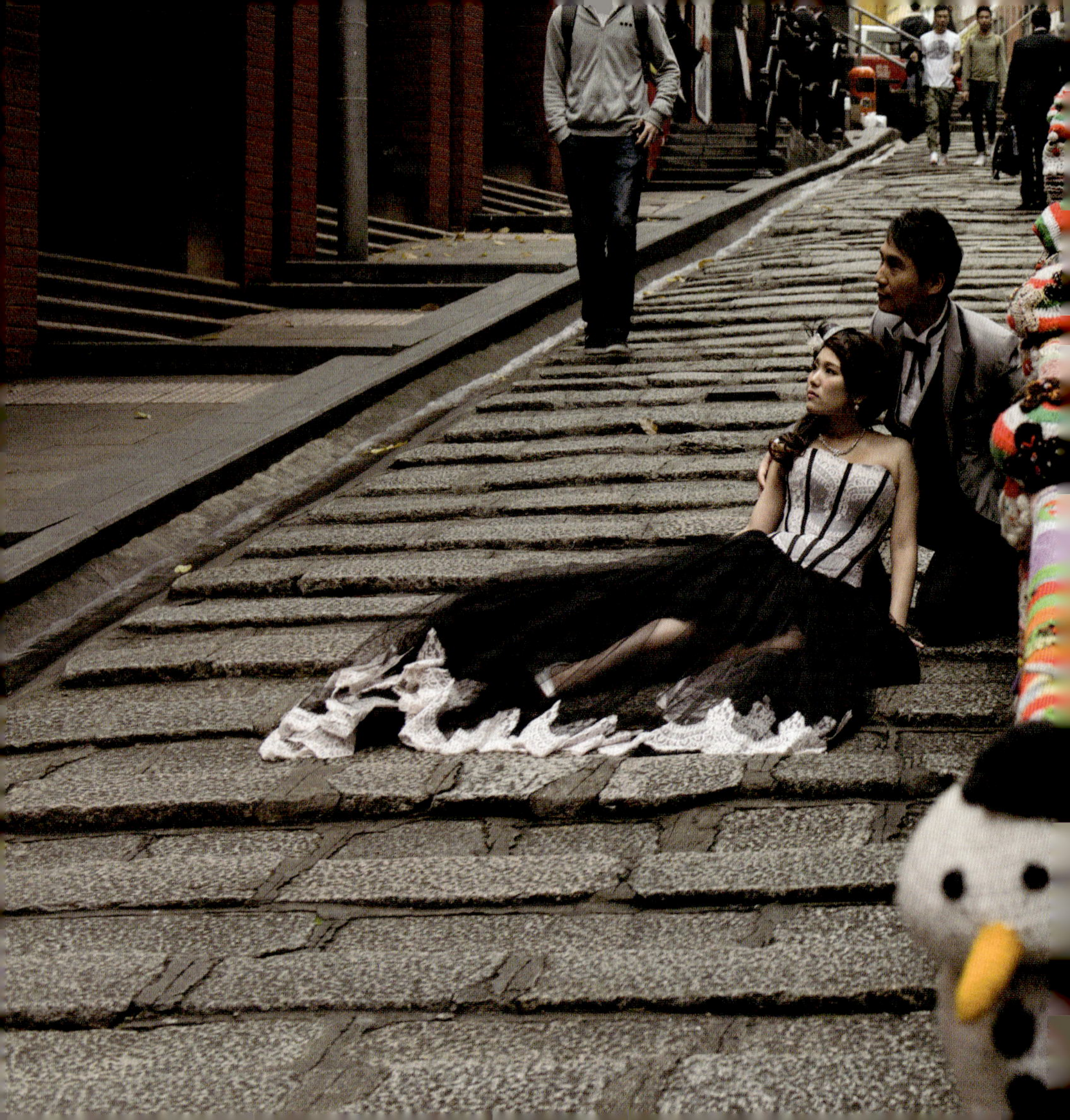

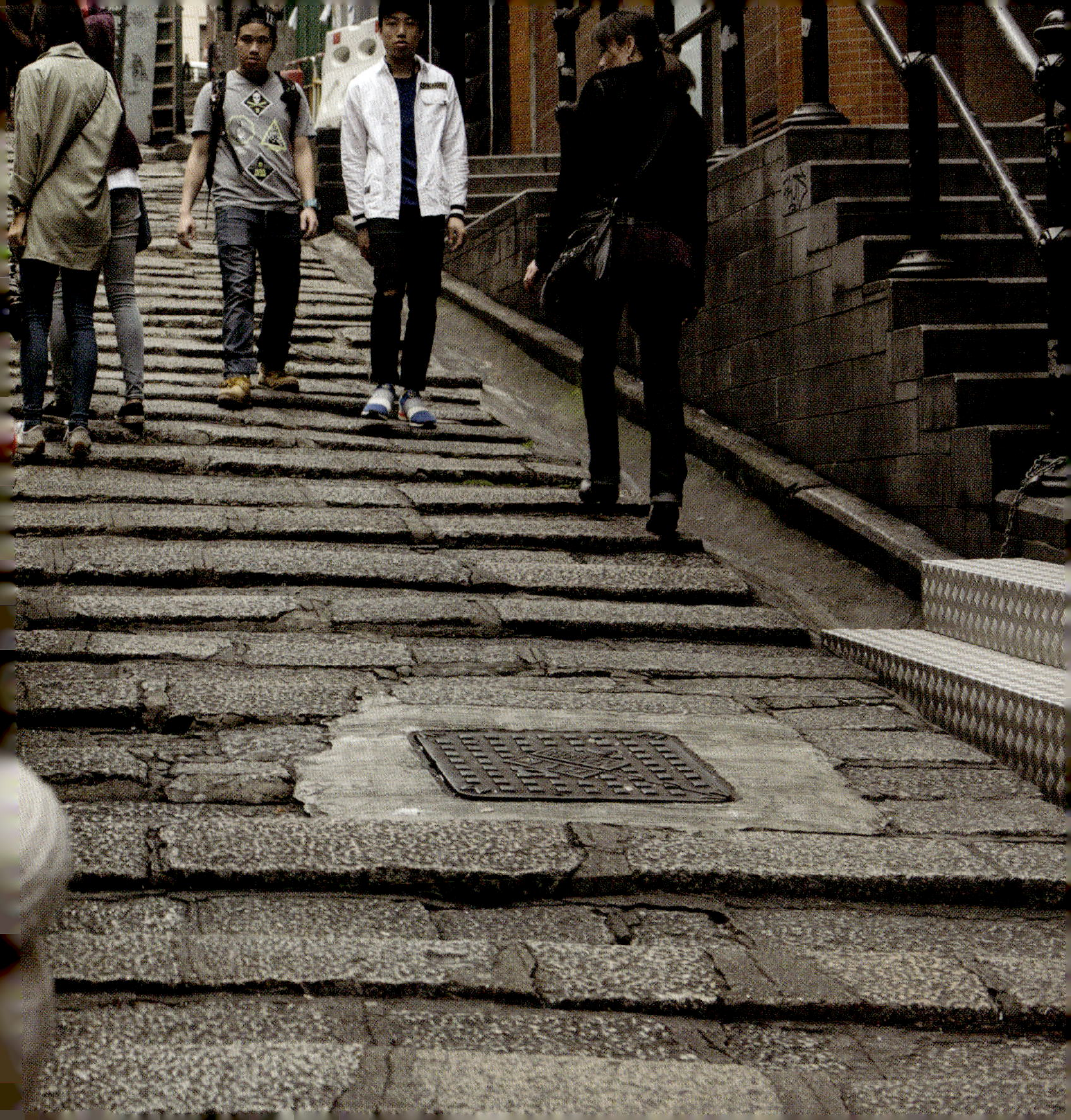

FASHION

Area: CENTRAL
35 Aberdeen Street

# PMQ

We can guarantee you haven't seen anything like this. What used to be the Police Married Quarters in the past, now is the most happening place with 7 levels of showrooms, boutiques, workshop spaces, creative offices and dining outlets. Interior, fashion, avant-garde jewelry and art – you name it, they have it. One cool thing about the PMQ project is that the young companies get their space rentals subsidised by government, which gives them an amazing opportunity to evolve and be discovered – by a random wanderer like yourself, or the rest of the world. Another cool thing is that the new life to the building was given by a $100 million donation made by a trio of local businessmen who support culture and call themselves 'Musketeers Education and Culture charitable foundation' – can't beat the romantics of this fact! Come and have a look in the daytime when all the shops are open or pop in the evening to get a bite of HK's social life – there is always some launching, tasting, lecture, workshop or just party, happening in here.

www.pmq.org.hk

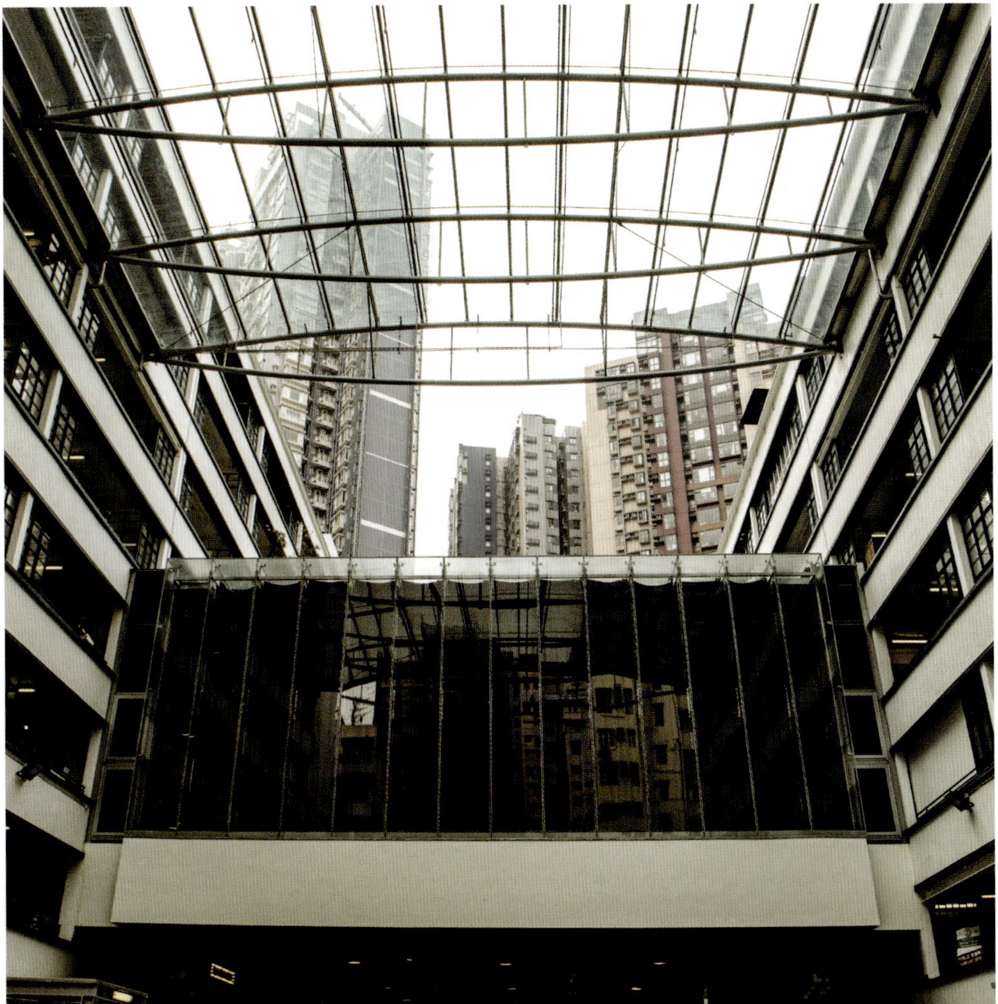

FASHION

Area: CENTRAL
11 Gough Street

# WOAW

Hipster's habitat: latest models of limited edition sneakers, cool little gadgets, niche perfumery and leather goods you won't find anywhere else. They don't call a store the "World Of Amazing Wonders" for no reason, you know. There is also a little coffee corner with a nice balcony – pop in for a long black. Leave with a pair of socks in a trending pattern.

www.woawstore.com

123

FASHION

Area: CENTRAL
Basement, No.27 Staunton Street

# LIANCA

Those studded belts and leather accessories displayed in the golden-lit window of the semi-basement shop look genuinely seductive, not to say sensually attractive. No. It's not an exclusive "adult shop" hiding in there. Just a fine leather boutique! Simple lines, striking colors, amazing quality – what else does a leather bag need, to look irresistibly hot? Maybe you, wearing it in style!

www.liancacentral.com

lianca
CENTRAL

FASHION

Area: CENTRAL
8 Elgin Street

# MARKIN

Planetary gear system rings, turbine and microchip cufflinks, suspension bridge ring, paperclip earrings – fine jewellery designer, Vladimir Markin is anything but shy when it comes to unleashing his creative force. Made of the top quality stones, gold and some other peculiar materials like ebony, these jewellery pieces are no less than a statement. Santa, do you copy?

www.vladimirmarkin.com

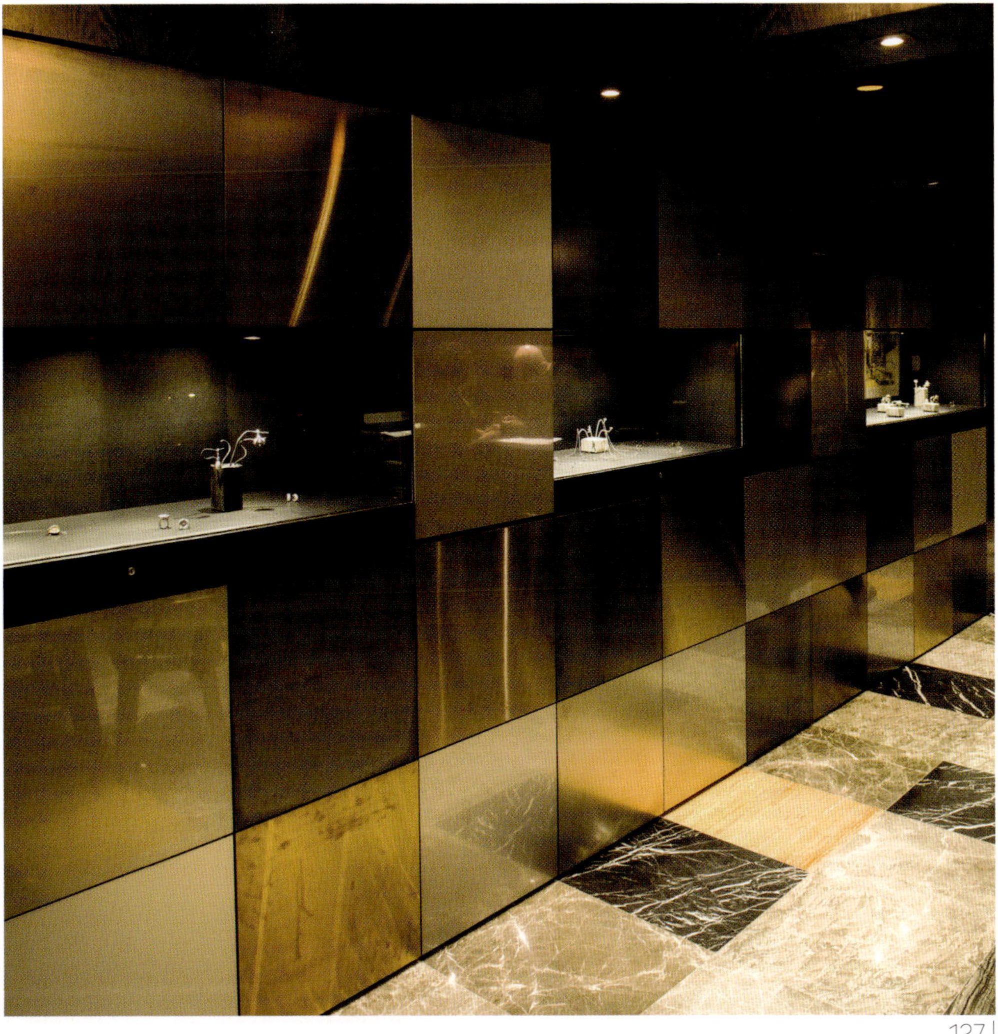

*FASHION*

Area: CENTRAL
16A Elgin Street

# JIMLLY JEWELRY

Leave your lady in this teeny-weeny shop and go get yourself a beer: she'll be stuck trying on the cutest silver lily pendants and ruby-clad butterfly earrings for a good thirty minutes. If you wear a skirt, you'll love this boutique.

www.facebook.com/jimllyjeweller

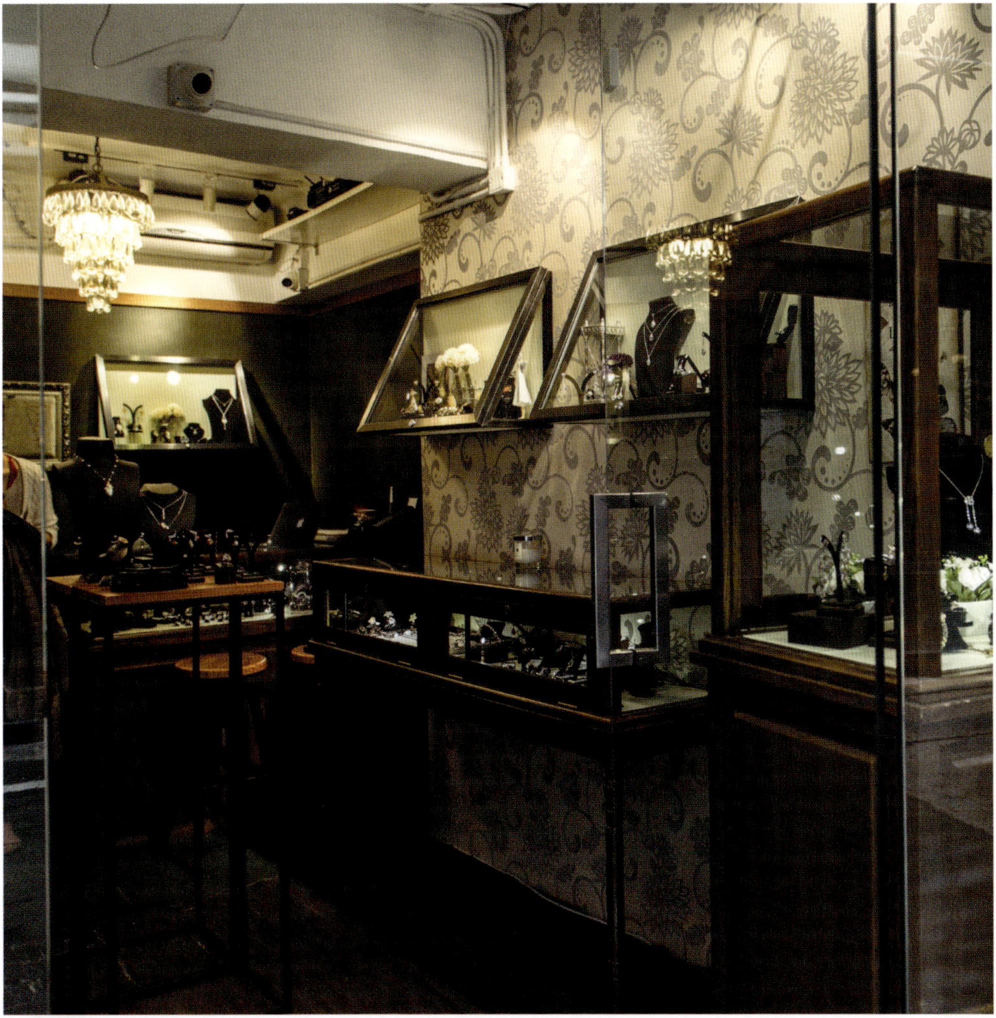

FASHION

Area: CENTRAL
G/F Man Yee Building

# INITIAL

This Hong Kong-born brand is playing tricks with the customers: the clothes are complex but minimalistic, bringing up Scandinavian, Japanese and peasant French motifs at the very same time. The stores take your breath away: the décor, textures, lighting and aromas are so artfully combined you can't believe there is no mistake when you look up the price at the hang tag. Yes. You can have it all!

www.initialfashion.com

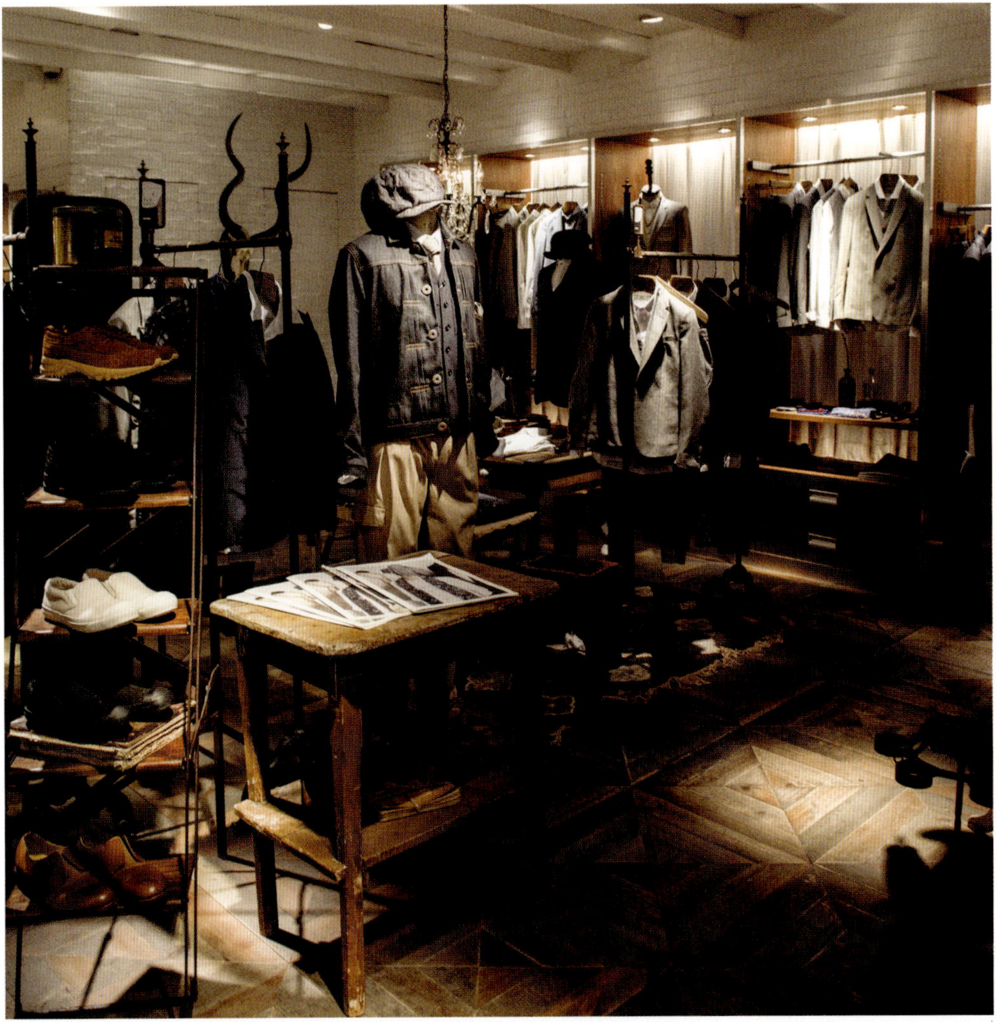

FASHION

Area: TAI PING SHAN
50 Po Hing Fong

# BROTHERS LEATHERCRAFT #50

The best souvenir from Hong Kong? The one you made with your own hands, of course! Get your hands on that piece of buttery cow leather: with just a one-day class you can learn how to make your own wallet or card holder. The craft workshops at this cosy friendly studio is a perfect idea for a rainy day, which can happen in this city, literally anytime.

www.facebook.com/brotherslc50

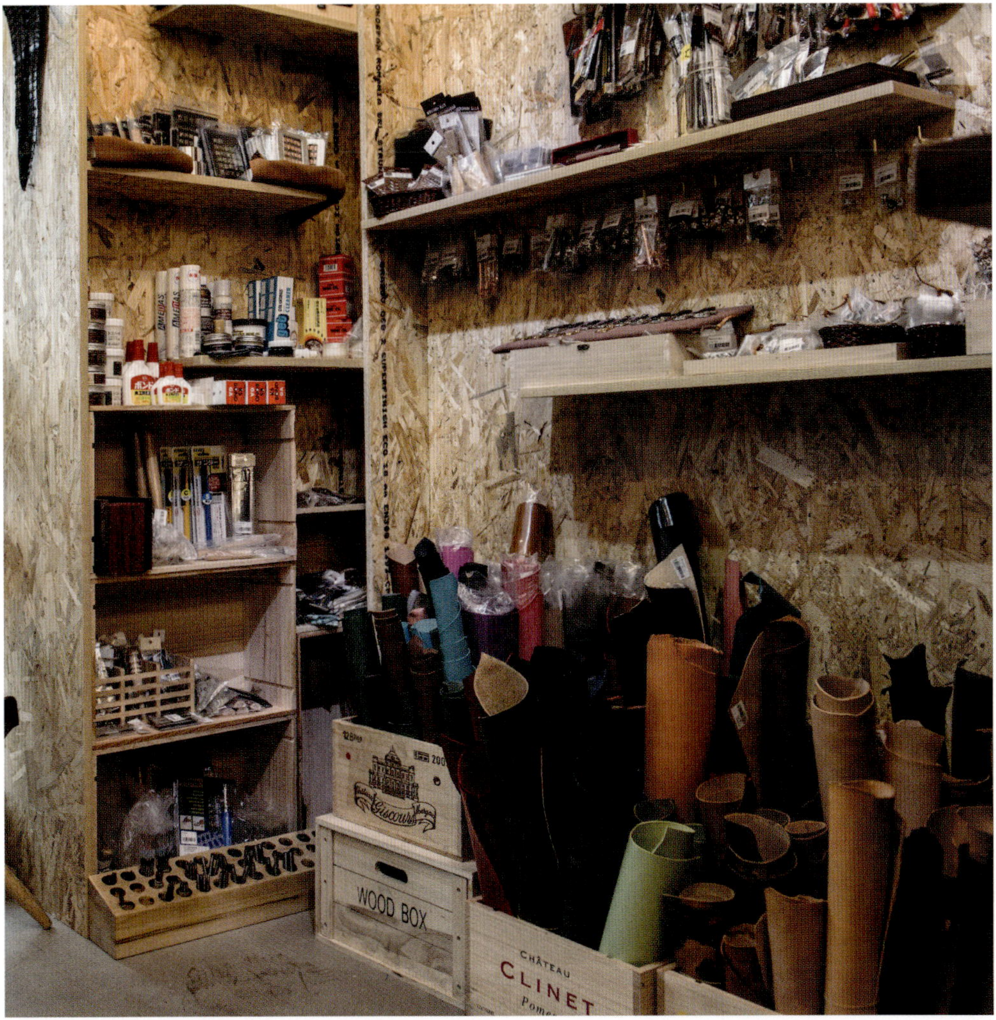
WOOD BOX
CHÂTEAU
CLINET

# INTERIOR DESIGN & DÉCOR

If you are not buying an apartment in Repulse Bay (although if you have a spare mil handy – you definitely should!), don't worry – take a piece of chic, cool and eclectic Hong Kong style back home and give it a nice style slap. Décor items, works of the young Chinese creative community, traditional Chinese objects or communism-soaked memorabilia – from modern and hot, to amusingly vulgar but fun, Hong Kong has it all.

Wander the little streets of Soho, searching for unusual finds. Go to the massive showrooms to get inspired, or zip down the alleys of PoHo, looking for hidden treasures. And yes, get that porcelain Mao at one of the Hollywood Rd stalls, selling antiques…of course you need it, and why? – Don't worry, you can worry about that later!

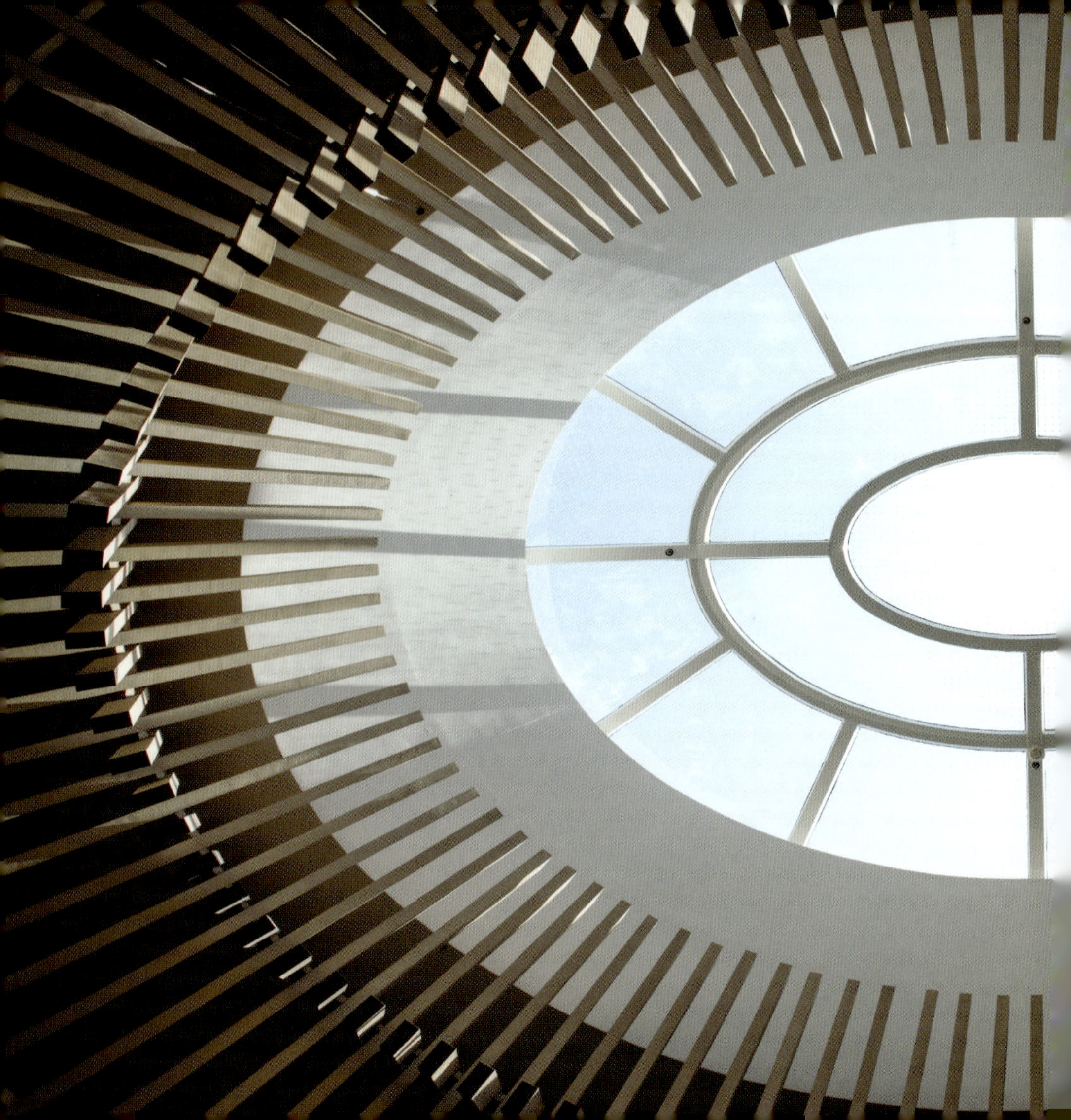

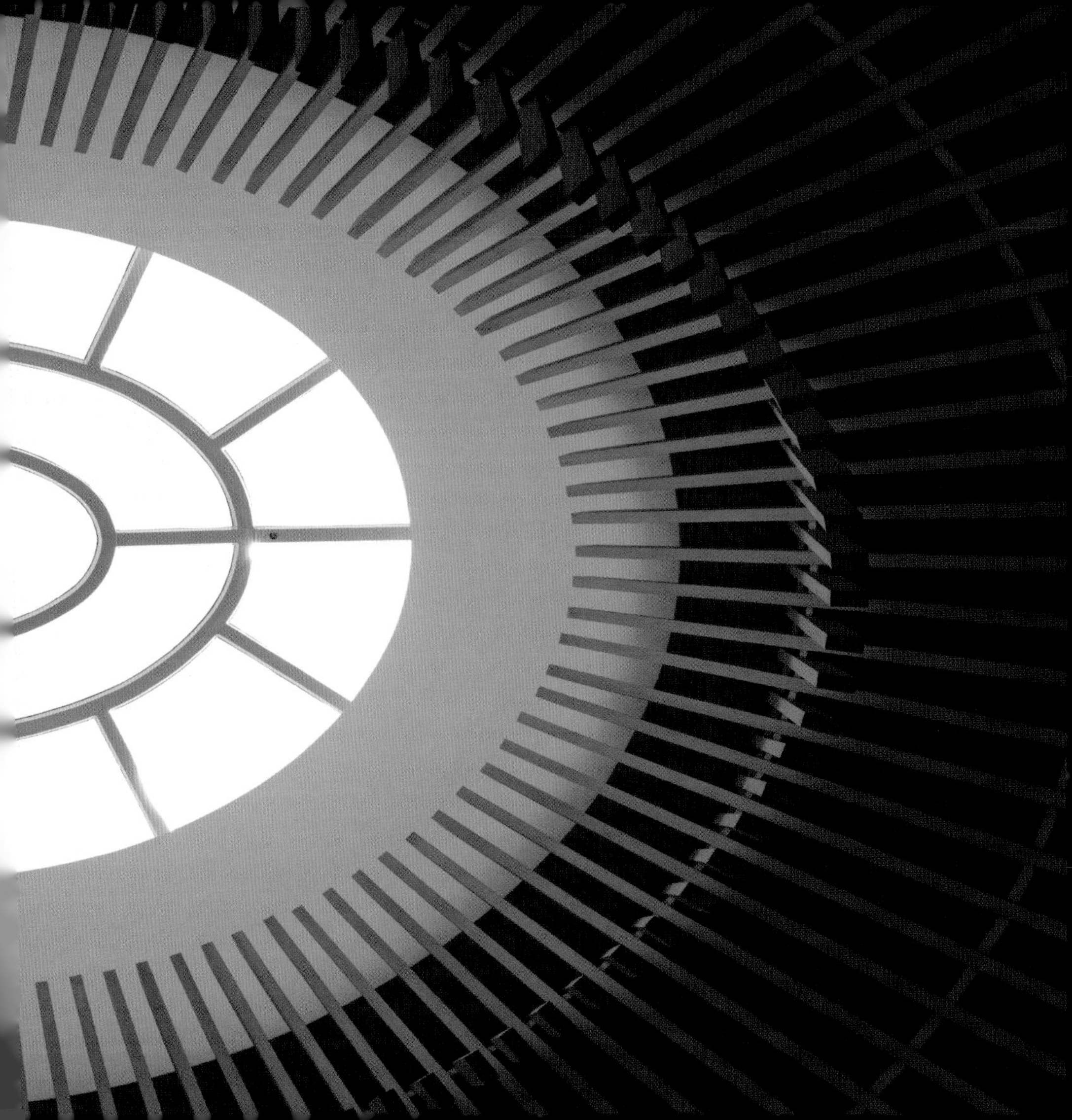

INTERIOR DESIGN & DÉCOR

Area: CENTRAL
G/F, Tung Tze Terrace 6 Aberdeen Street

# GREENFINGERS' ACADEMY

Known for their bespoke wedding flower decors, this high-end studio can brighten up even the less important day of your life: order your precious self a sublime bouquet of baby blue roses and get out of the blues. Or take you passion for flowers even further by joining the Green Fingers' Academy, which will introduce you to the basics of modern floral design. Flower power!

www.greenfingers.com.hk

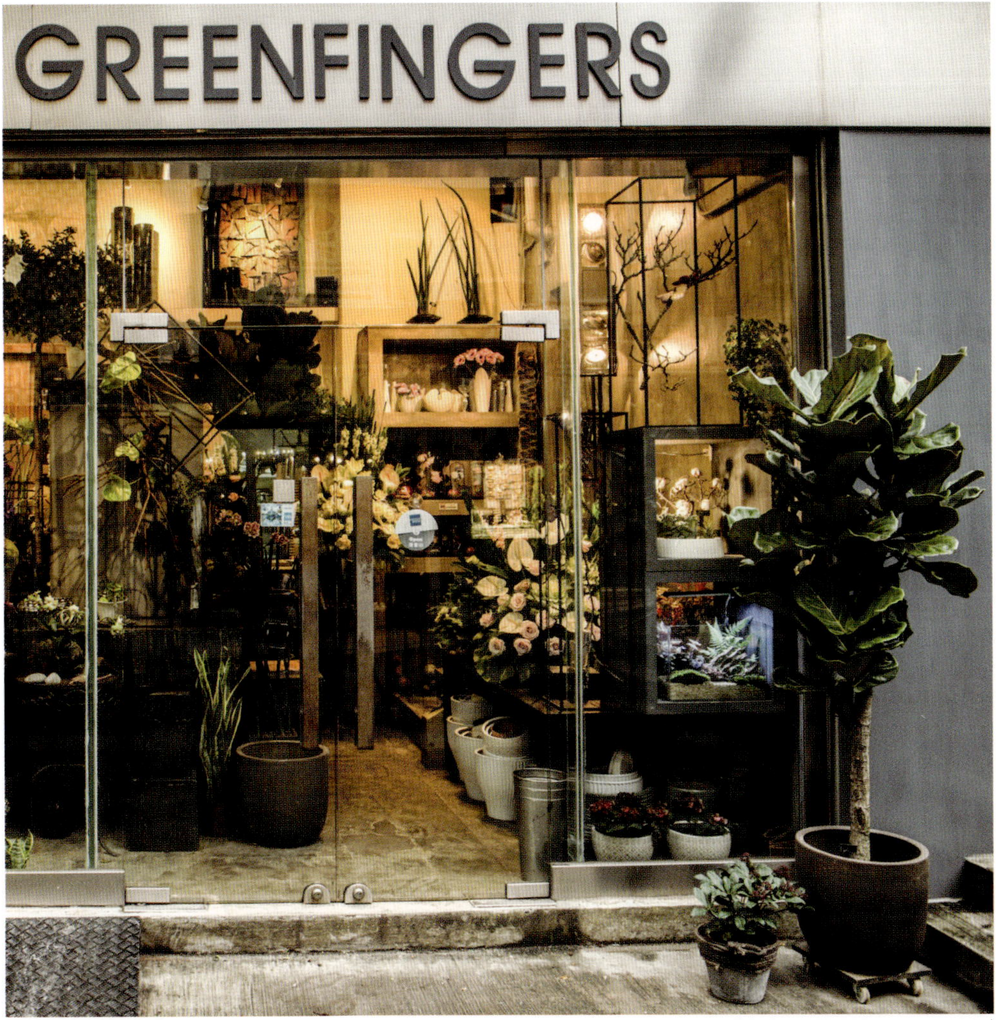
GREENFINGERS

INTERIOR DESIGN & DÉCOR

Area: CENTRAL
49 Hollywood Road

# HOME ESSENTIALS

Looking for a neon elk's head for your wall, giant pitbull cushion, pottery that would fit Mad Hatter's tea party or something less flamboyant but yet, twisted enough to make the plainest interior look like a street artist's pad? Look no further.

www.HomeEssentials.com.hk

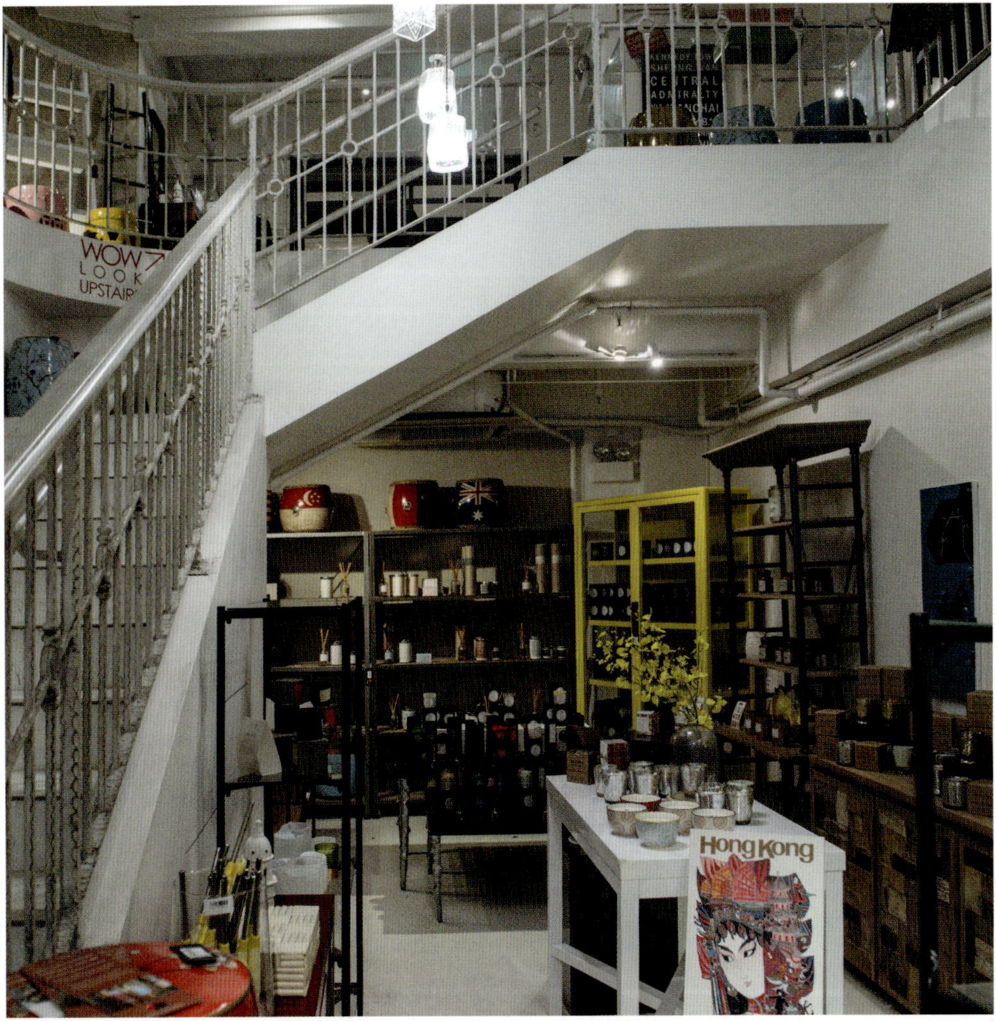
WOW
LOOK
CENTRAL
ADMIRALTY
Hong Kong

INTERIOR DESIGN & DÉCOR

Area: CENTRAL & WAN CHAI
17 Gough Street, Central & 15 St Francis Street, Wan Chai

# TIMOTHY OULTON

This is the house of a man you'd rather be – or whom you'd rather be with. Everything screams gentleman's cave here: cushy sofas handcrafted from rich leather in dark chocolate, heavy retro suitcases piled in the corner, leather hides draped on the wall. Sean Connery would look right in place in here. Don't be surprised if you'll be served a glass of champagne, (even if it's 11am and you are not even buying a thing) – that's how gentlemen do it!

www.timothyoulton.com

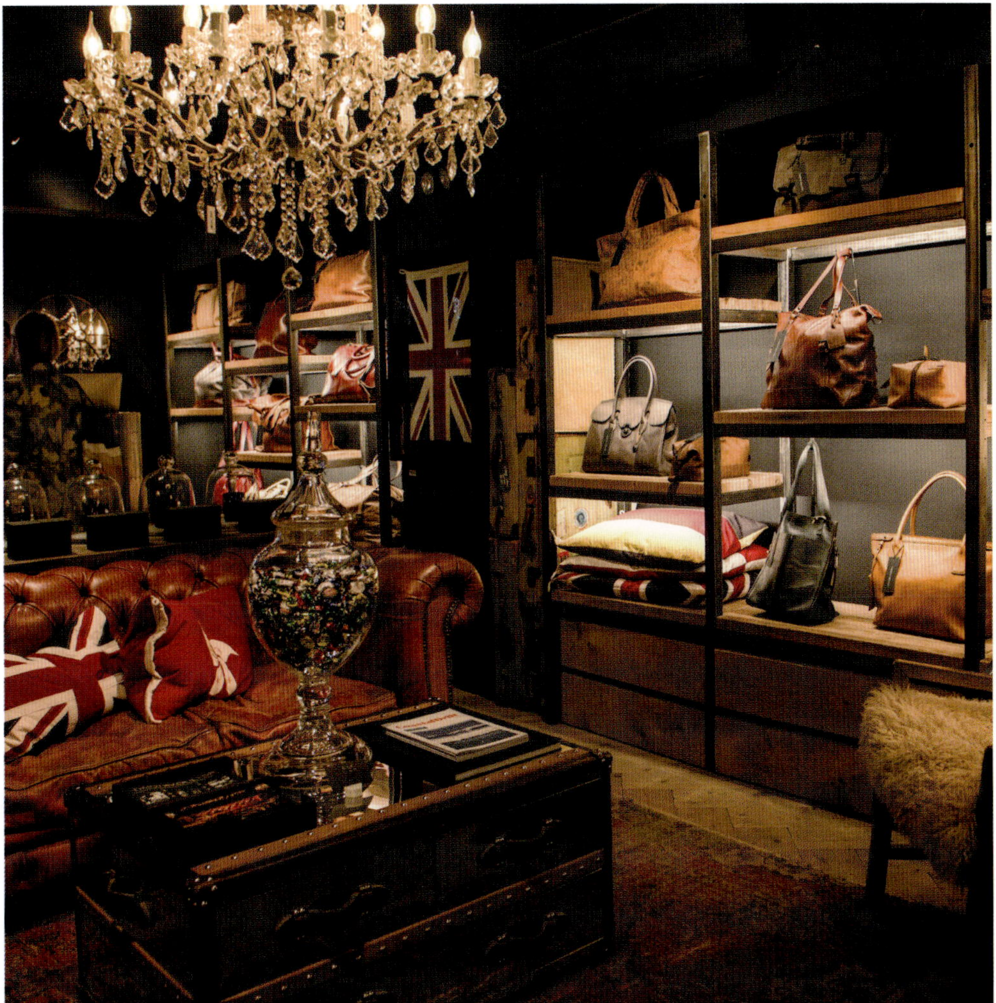

Area: SHEUNG WAN

# HOLLYWOOD ROAD

Hollywood Road is one cool street. It can be a bar hopping place, an art lover's paradise, a shopping destination or a gold mine for the treasure hunters – or maybe everything at once. At one end of it there are watering holes for blue collars and clubs for the neversleeping crowd, then the middle part is packed with great shops and lovely art galleries and the very end of the street is famous for it's antiques shop: every second door leads to a treasury. There are shops selling vintage porcelain statuettes (everyone needs a miniature fragile Mao, right?), art pieces made of carved mammoth horns, old China memorabilia like the silly pink piggybanks, and tons of jade. If you are looking for treasure, get ready to dig in tons of crap. But a leisure walk on the sunny day at the little pedestrian appendix with the stalls piled with curiosities is always a great idea anyways.

145

INTERIOR DESIGN & DÉCOR

Area: SHEUNG WAN
Ground Floor, 56 Sai Street

# AMELIE & TULIPS

2-level showroom featuring furniture and décor elements that are fun yet classy, and very practical, too. It's all about some great brands with the magic ability to turn any interior into a designer space: Christopher Boots, &Tradition, Carl Hansen&Son, Barcelona Design, Christian Haas, Stellar Works. With nothing too trendy or over-the-top crazy all the objects displayed here have this charm that's hard to resist. Get yourself a designer coffee table for your growing collection of Define Fine books!

www.amelieandtulips.com

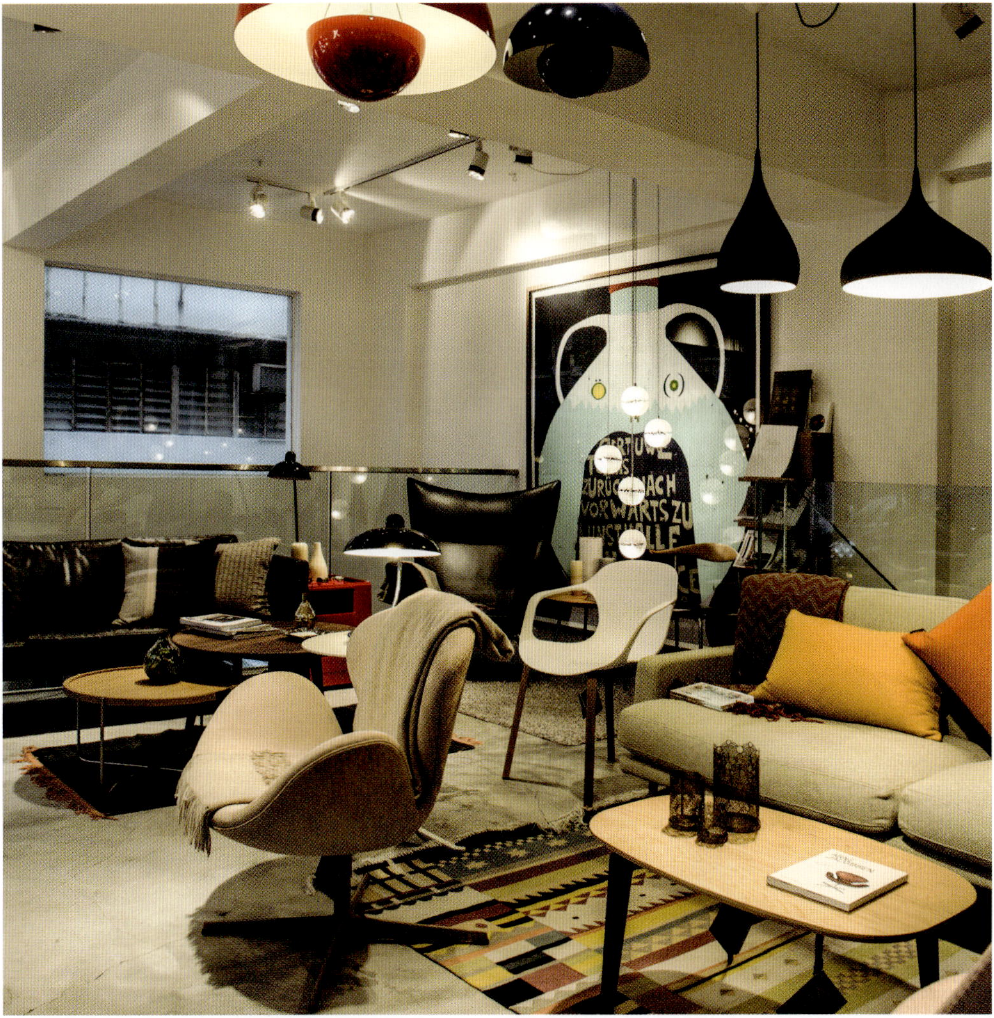
VORWARTS ZU

INTERIOR DESIGN & DÉCOR

Area: CAUSEWAY BAY
95 Leighton Road

# LOVERAMICS

Everyone's cup of love: pretty pottery for any occasion - modern, cute and fun. Mind you, you'd like to touch and feel every second cup, and so you should. Naïve and childish or sleek and all grown-up, mat or glossy, glazed or rough, decorated with the fairytale motifs or elegant in simplicity – all those coffee mugs, bowls, saucers and plates are just adorable. Liberty in London and at MoMA in New York that sell Loveramics apparently think so, too. Pimp your cupboard!

www.loveramics.com

149

INTERIOR DESIGN & DÉCOR

Area: CENTRAL
Horizon Plaza, 2 Lee Wing St

# TEQUILA KOLA

A to Z of the chic, yet funky lifestyle: Chesterfield sofas in turquoise plush, chevron-patterned cushions, vintage rugs and cheeky home assessories to bring a smile to anyone's face. The best thing? They deliver worldwide!

www.tequilakola.com

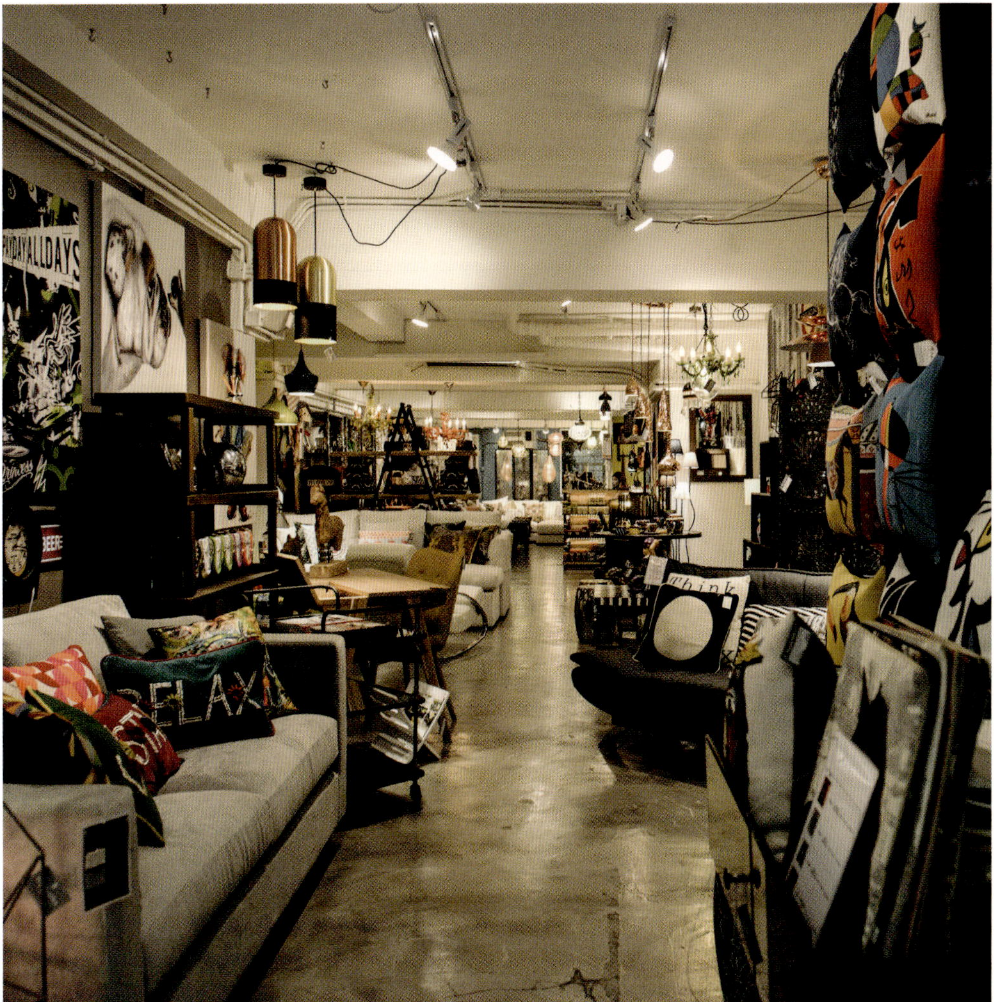

INTERIOR DESIGN & DÉCOR

Area: CENTRAL
28/F, Horizon Plaza, 2 Lee Wing Street, Ap Lei Chau

# TREE

Knock on wood! Beautiful teak reigns here: it's impossible to stop caressing those cabinets and tabletops. We love this "eco-wood" company not only for making the interiors prettier, but also for their consciousness: these guys have collaborated with many charities for the past years and have planted over 70.000 trees – now we are talking about the art of giving back!

www.tree.com.hk

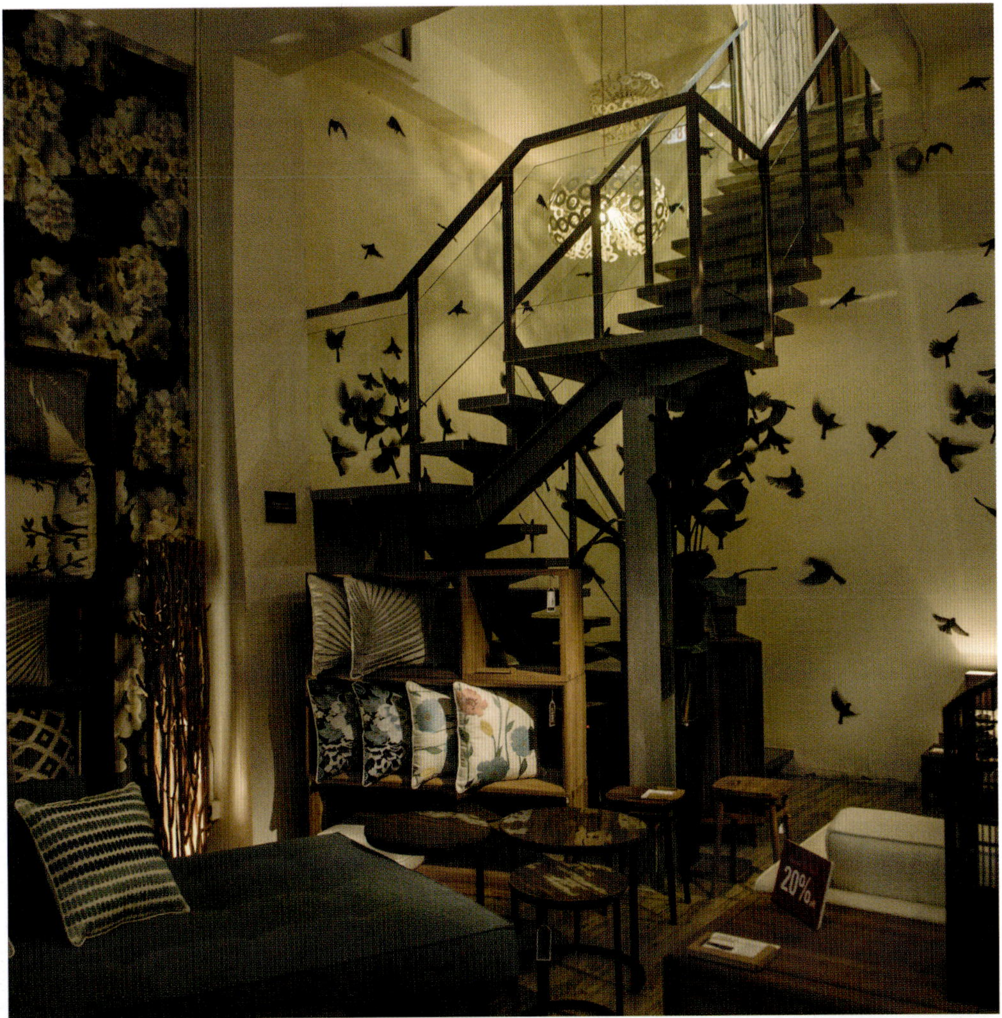
20%

# HEALTH & BEAUTY

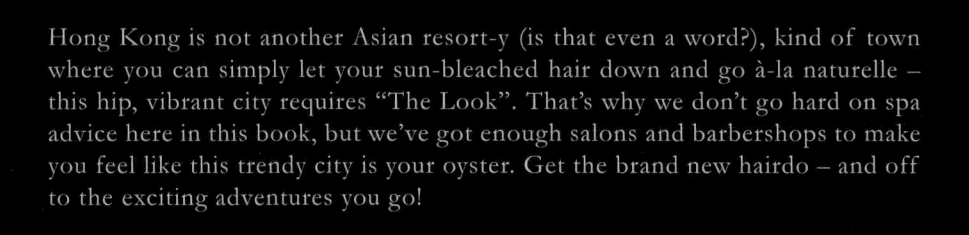

Hong Kong is not another Asian resort-y (is that even a word?), kind of town where you can simply let your sun-bleached hair down and go à-la naturelle – this hip, vibrant city requires "The Look". That's why we don't go hard on spa advice here in this book, but we've got enough salons and barbershops to make you feel like this trendy city is your oyster. Get the brand new hairdo – and off to the exciting adventures you go!

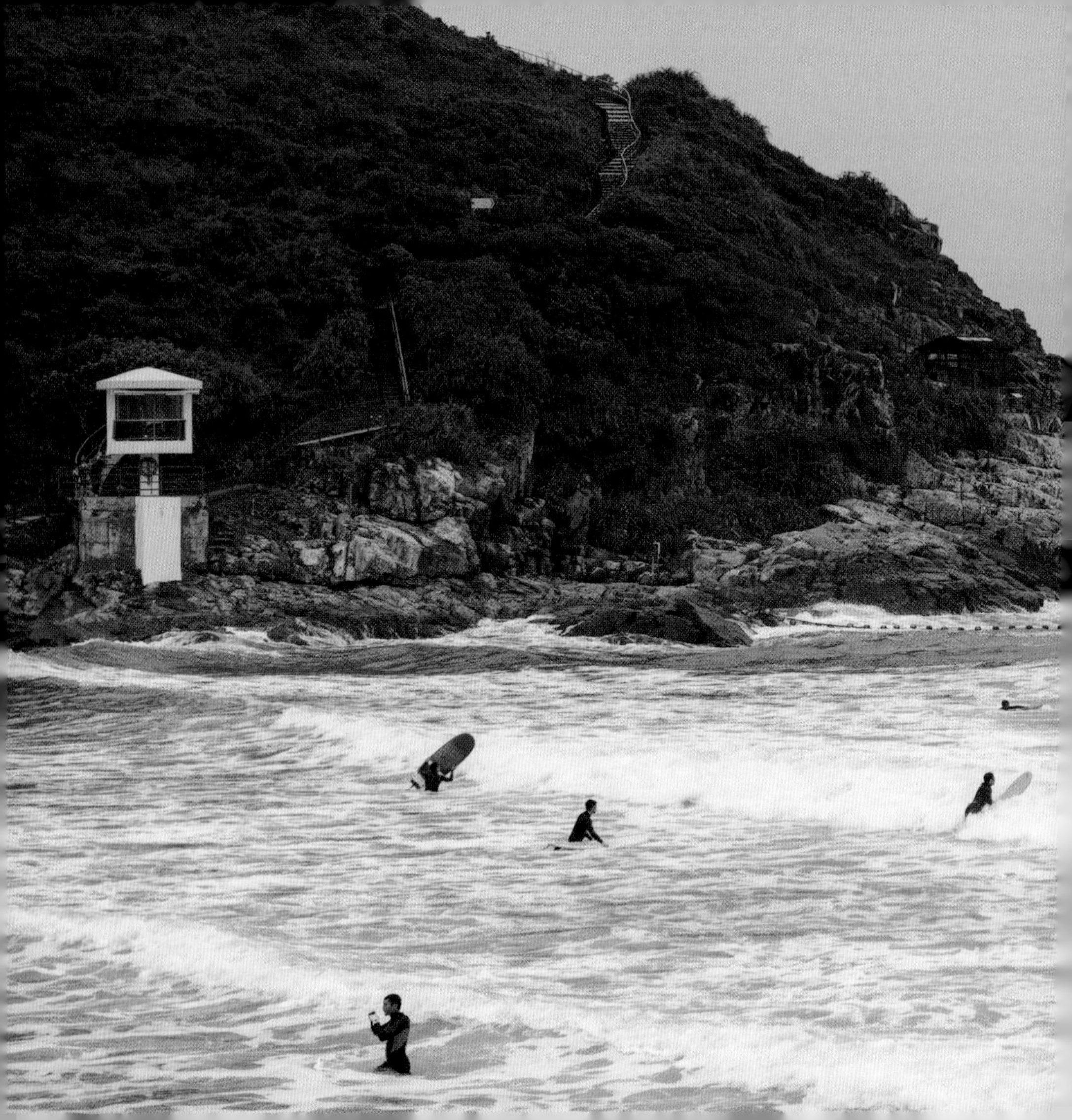

HEALTH & BEAUTY

Area: CENTRAL
Albany Road

# HONG KONG
# Zoological and Botanical gardens

After a few days in the concrete jungle, which Hong Kong is, you will be desperate for a bit of nature. Thank God, you don't need to travel far: the oasis of lush vegetation is almost in the city centre. Fountains, shady nooks, sculptures and birds singing cheerfully – this park built in the Victorian era is a perfect place to get an oxygen superdose, rosy cheeks and some pretty tan.

www.lcsd.gov.hk/tc/parks/hkzbg

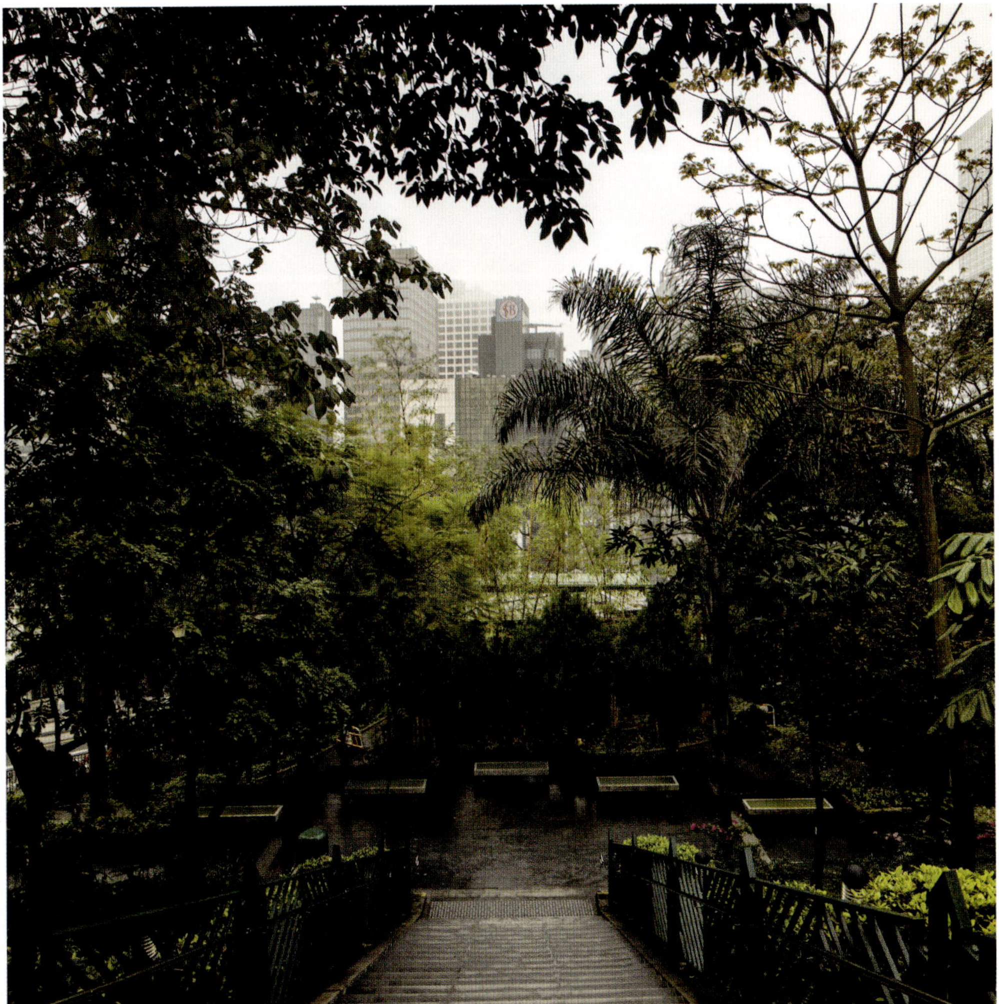

HEALTH & BEAUTY

Area: CENTRAL
1/F 18 Cochrane

# THE STRAND

The beauty empire within one building: one floor for him, one floor for her, another one for spa treatments and the rooftop for flicking your freshly done hair while sipping on the bubbly. World-class stylists from all around the globe, and prices to match.

www.thestrandhk.com

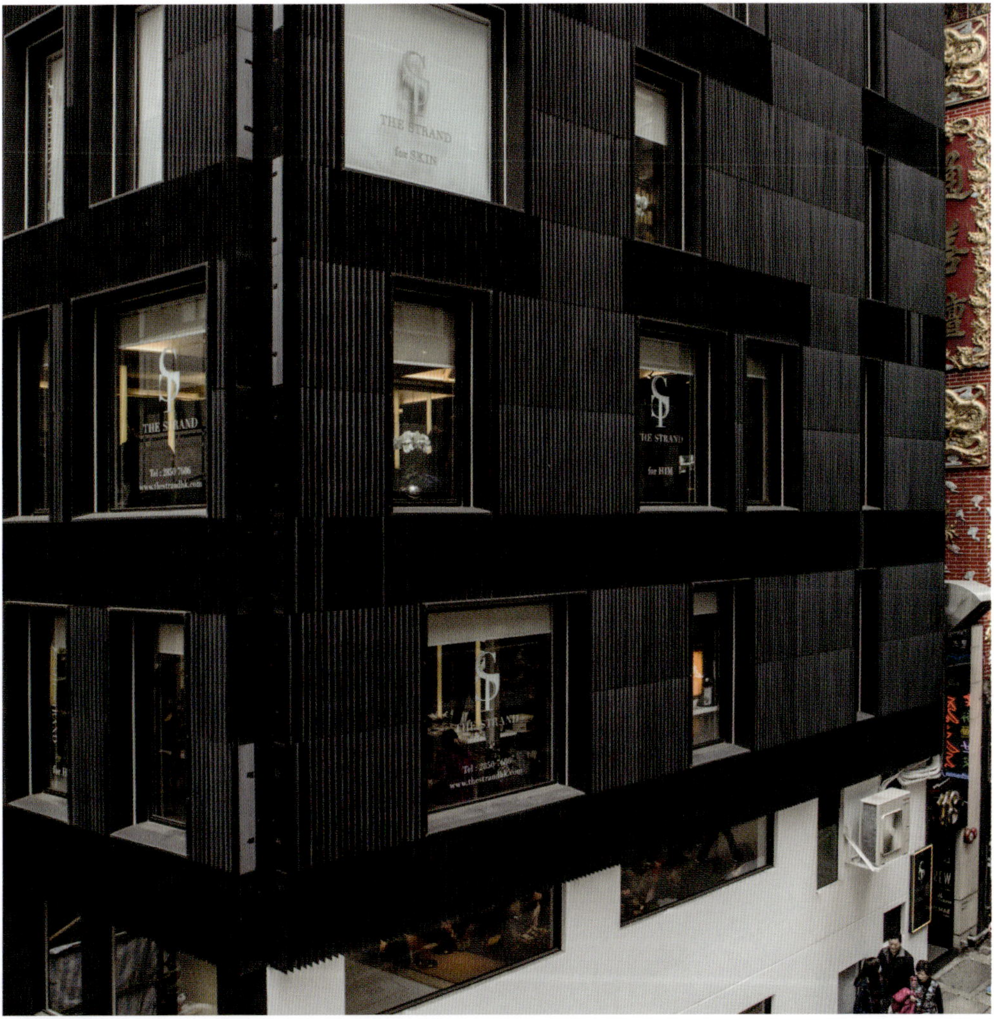
THE STRAND
for SKIN
THE STRAND
THE STRAND
for HIM

HEALTH & BEAUTY

Area: CENTRAL
16/F 11 Stanley St

# BEYORG

A spot not only for organic and non-toxic beauty products but for some indulgent and hi-end spa treatments, too. Go for a stimulating, firm Swedish massage and then melt away during one of the lavish facial rituals. Heaven.

www.beyorgbeauty.com

WE KEEP IT FRESH

SPA

HEALTH & BEAUTY

Area: CENTRAL
43-49 Wellington St

# GENTLEMEN'S TONIC

Walk in as a mere bloke, walk out as Don Draper. Magic!

www.gentlemenstonic.com

GENTLEMEN'S
TONIC
MAYFAIR

HEALTH & BEAUTY

Area: SHEUNG WAN
Shop 1, G/F, Po Hing Court 10-18

# RAY CHAN HAIR SALON

Hair cut by Wong Kar-wai's favorite hairstylist? Yes, please! Ray Chan has been working with the world-famous Hong Kong movie director on the set of "In The Mood For Love" and other beautiful flicks, now you can have him styling your head at his own bohemian salon-cum-artspace-cum-vintage gallery in the coolest neighborhood of PoHo. Wander in, even if you don't need a cut: it's a treasury box with lots of curiosities on display, and the owner is always ready for a good chat.

www.facebook.com/chkchan

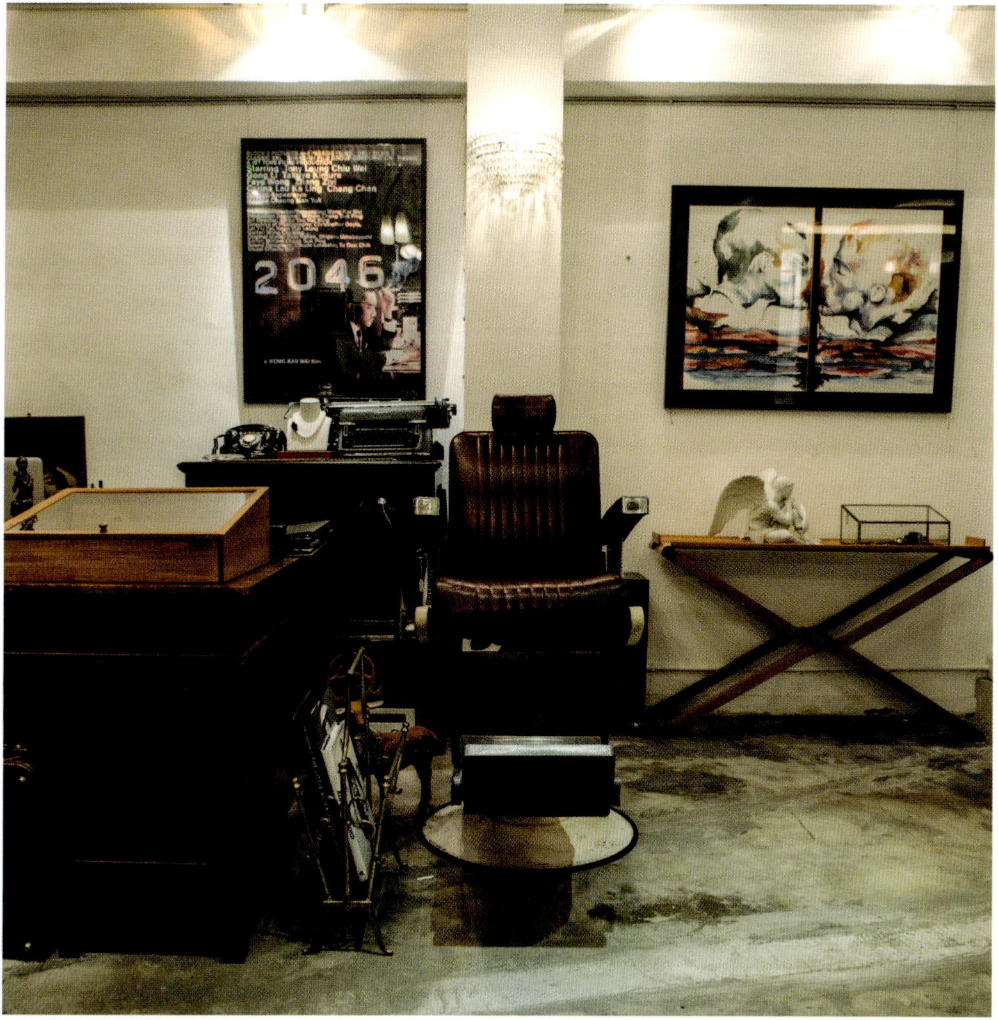
2046

HEALTH & BEAUTY

Area: CENTRAL
41-43 Graham Street

# FOX AND THE BARBER

Grooming HQ! Beard trims, "dangerous" blade shaves, imported grooming products coming all the way from London and the US and a skillful redhead barber at your service…everything to turn a beast into a man-beauty.

www.foxandthebarber.com

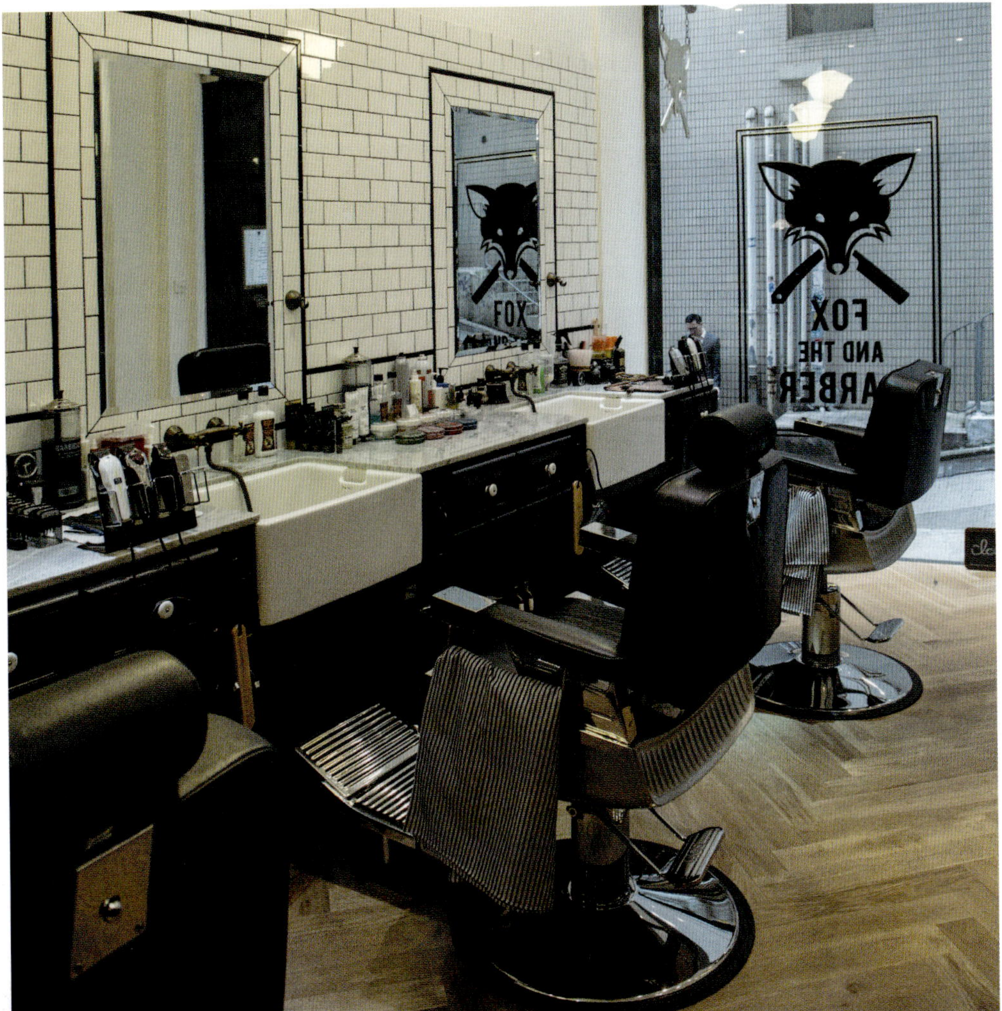
FOX
AND THE

ADVENTURE

much happening here! Parties, art fairs, gallery launches, food tastings – you'll probably need the latest time management app to get the most out of this place! But it's not only about the big city fun. Hong Kong is truly full of surprises – think virgin-looking beaches, bare foot BBQs, boating under the scarlet sails and tours to the serial maniac's cave…well, almost!

There is so much to do in this city that we haven't even tried to cover it all. Instead, we've picked a bunch of our all-time favourites and served it to you on a platter, just as a starting point of exploration.

The rest is in your own hands – and we are sure you won't let us down!

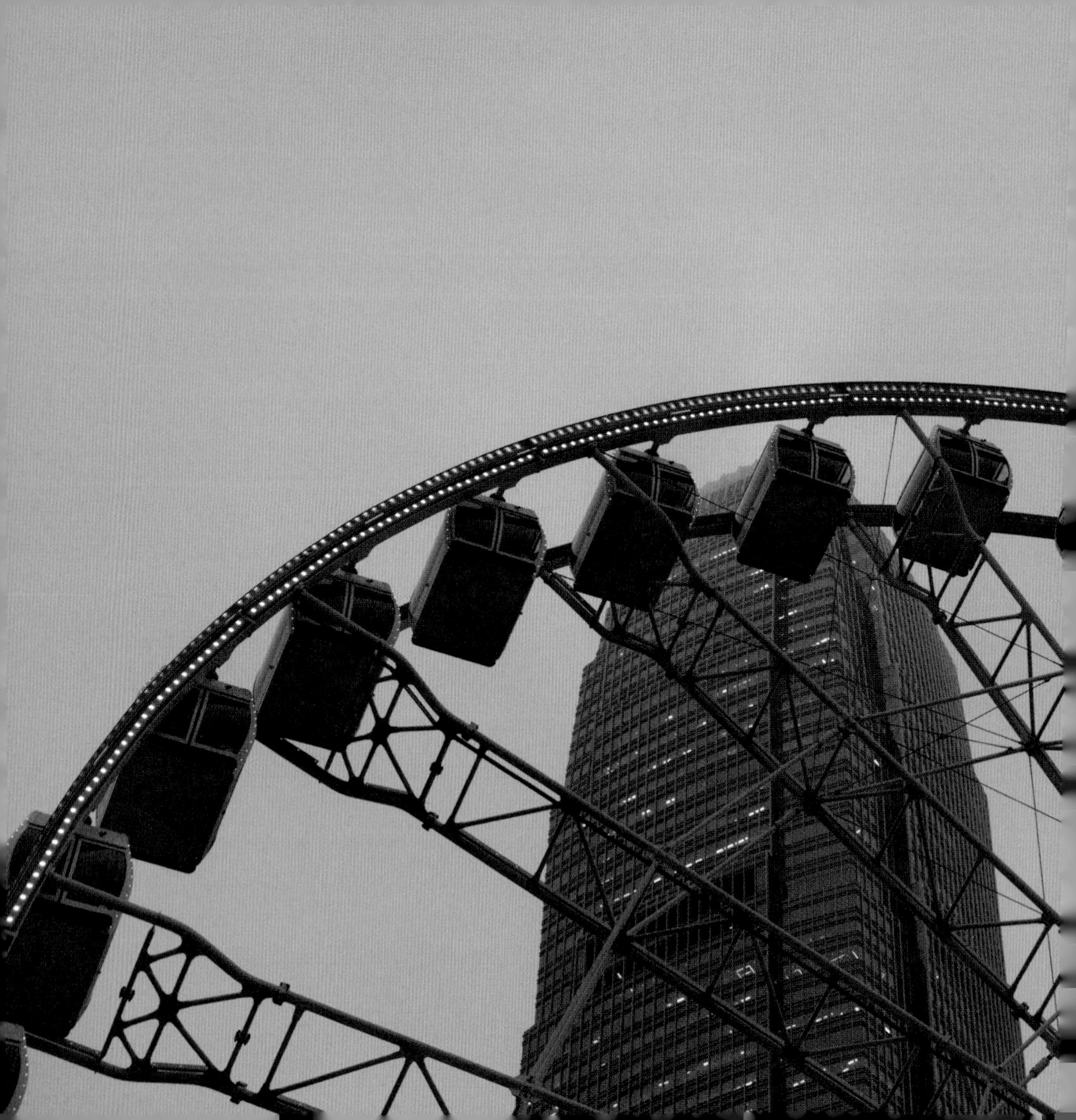

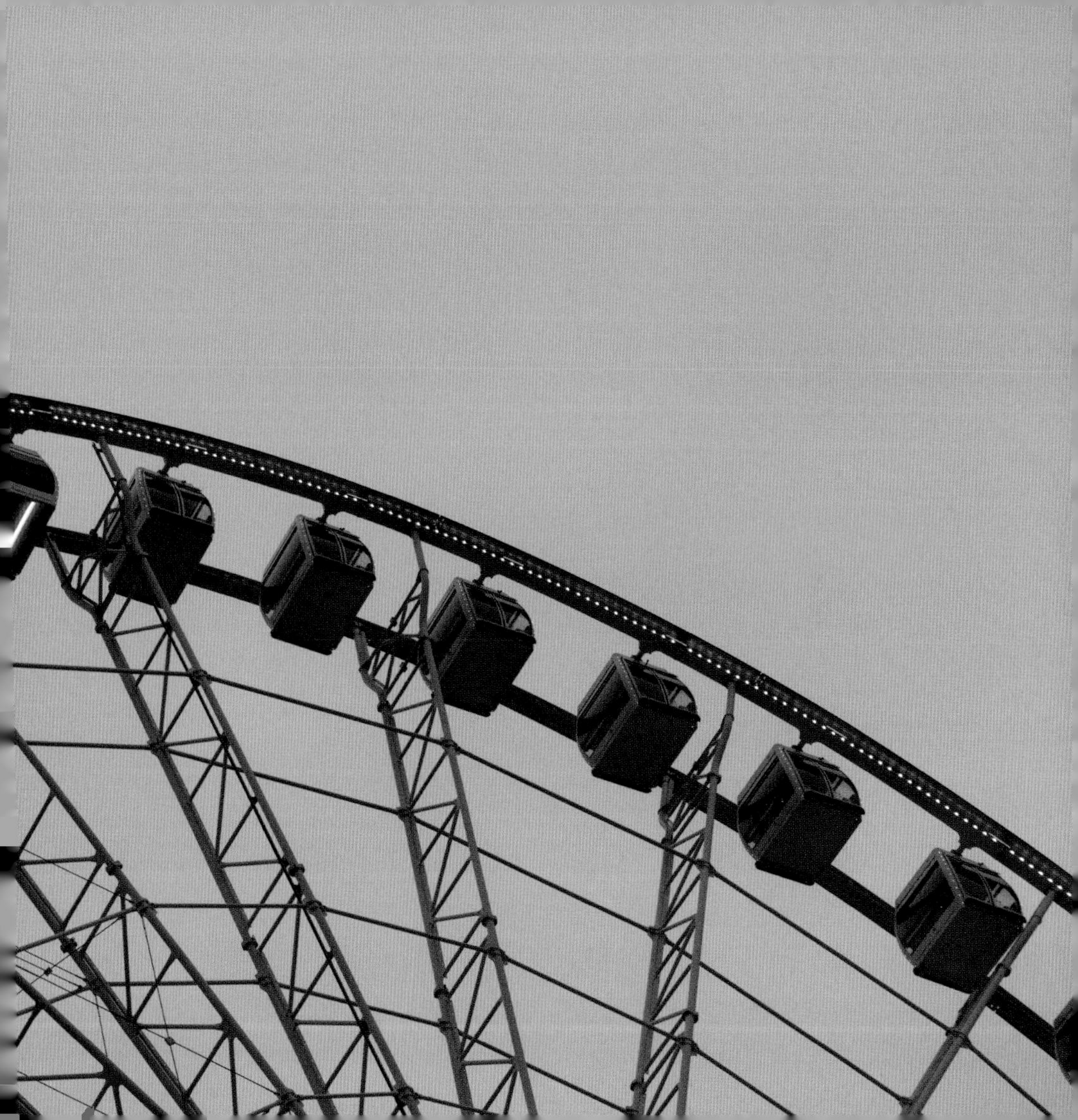

ADVENTURE

Area: CENTRAL
Central Pier No. 9

# AQUALUNA JUNK BOAT

Sail away with me, honey! What can be more romantic than the scarlet sails popping up against the grayish foggy background of Hong Kong island is skyline? The traditional junk boat looks like a treasure hunter, while being a true gem itself.

www.aqualuna.com.hk

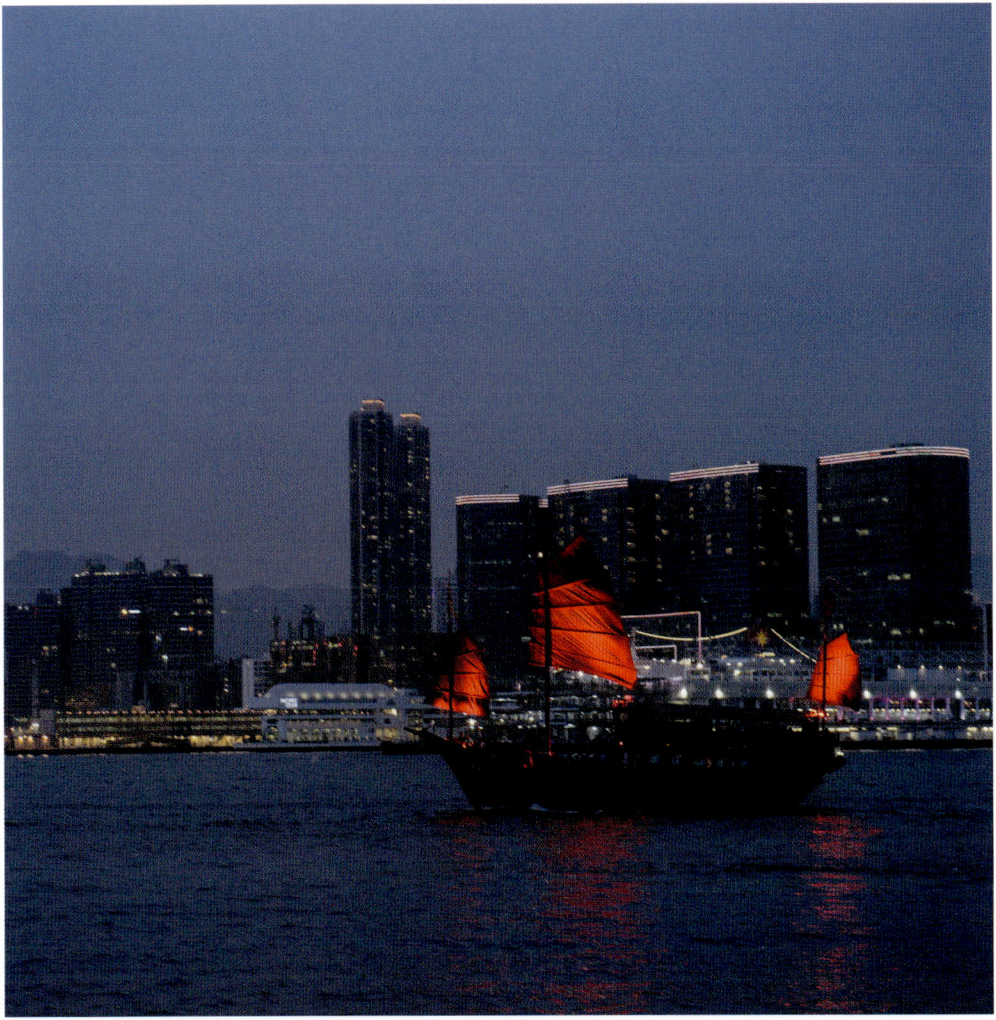

ADVENTURE

# STANLEY

A weekend staple. Pick a sunny day, take a double-decker bus for the best views (strictly top floor sitting!), bring your dog, your kids, your lover and blend in with the weekend crowd. Avoid the market as plague. Have a leisurely stroll and then retire at one of the promenade's bars for well-deserved beers, burgers and fish & chips in a merry company of HK expats. Done? Move to Sheck O for a different kind of beach experience.

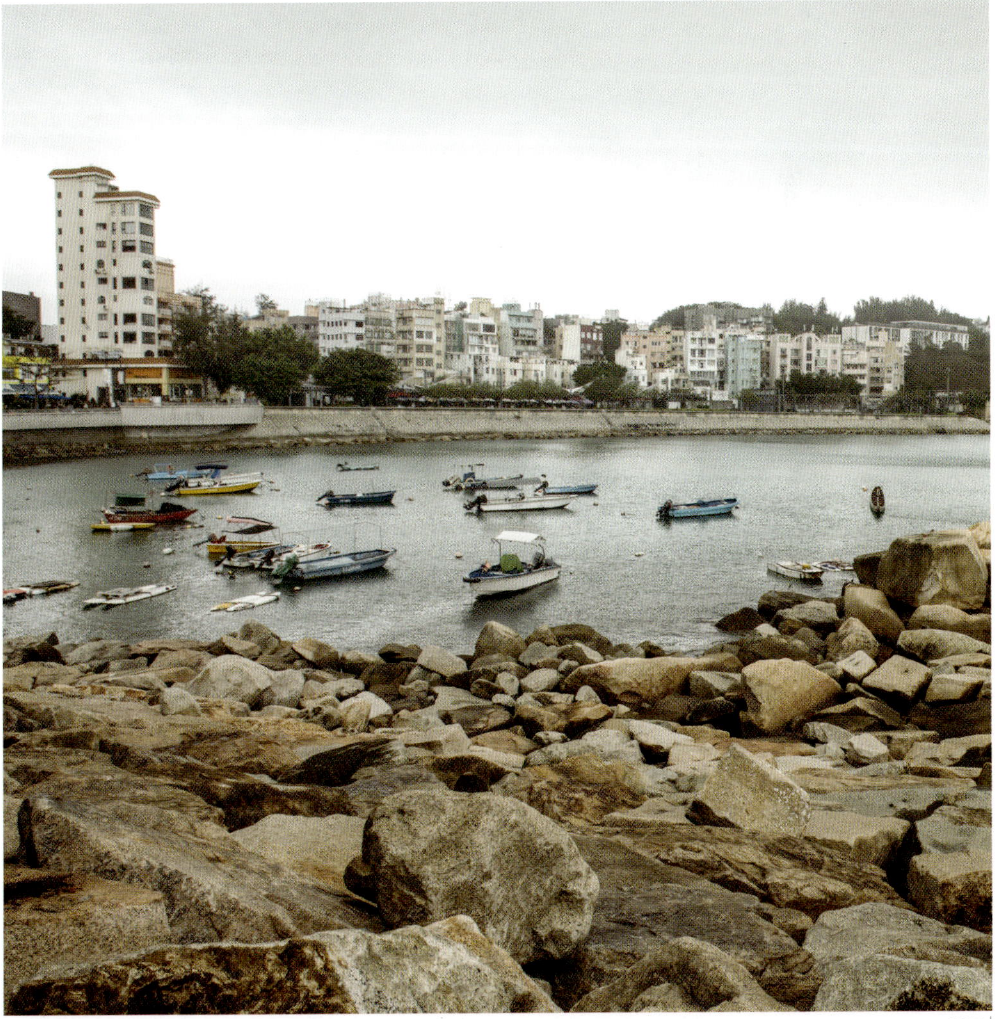

ADVENTURE

# BIG WAVE BAY

Surfing beach, surfers' village, surfing everything. Big chill. Stunning landscape.

179

ADVENTURE

Area: SHEUNG WAN
Po Hing Fong 72

# HONG KONG MUSEUM OF MEDICAL SCIENCE

Get ready for that "American Horror Story" experience: this pretty heritage mansion contains some proper horror movie props like an antique dentist chair, surgery table and some tools that would be appreciated by Hannibal Lector – all stored in a dimmed basement, of course. Sit back for a little movie telling the story of the IX century's massive plague epidemic, and how it kick-started the modern days medicine science in Asia. Explore the hip neighborhood of PoHo after the trip to the past – you'll need a good cuppa after what you've seen!

www.hkmms.org.hk/en

香港醫學博物館
Hong Kong Museum of Medical Sciences

ADVENTURE

# REPULSE BAY

Opposite to the ever-busy Hong Kong city, this neighborhood has a completely different vibe of a resort town. Idyllic beach, golf, destination spa, rooftop drinks with that ocean view and all the new, cool dining spots that keep popping up like mushrooms after a rain – Repulse Bay is one trending hood these days. Explore with no rush. Come for a day of art therapy at the famous creative hub, Anastassia's Art House, shop away at the brand new, ultramodern mall The Pulse…or simply stroll along the promenade enjoying a sunny day. Life is a beach, after all!

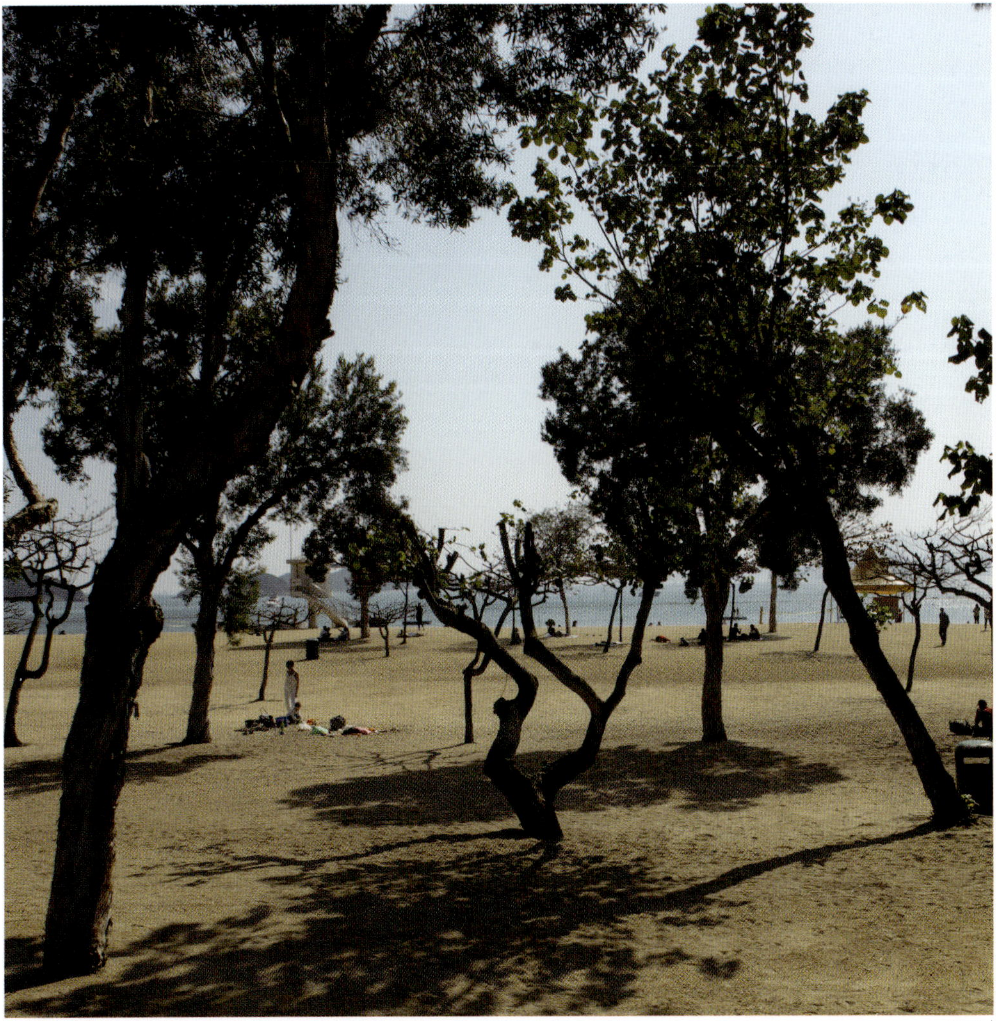

ADVENTURE

# LAMMA ISLAND

Get away from the big city buzz, hop on the ferry and get a bite of the island life pleasures. Disembark at the quiet shores of Lamma, have a nice walk around the vivid village, see the temples, watch the fishermen sorting their catch and then dive into a plate of the grilled seafood this island is famous for. Can't be better than that.

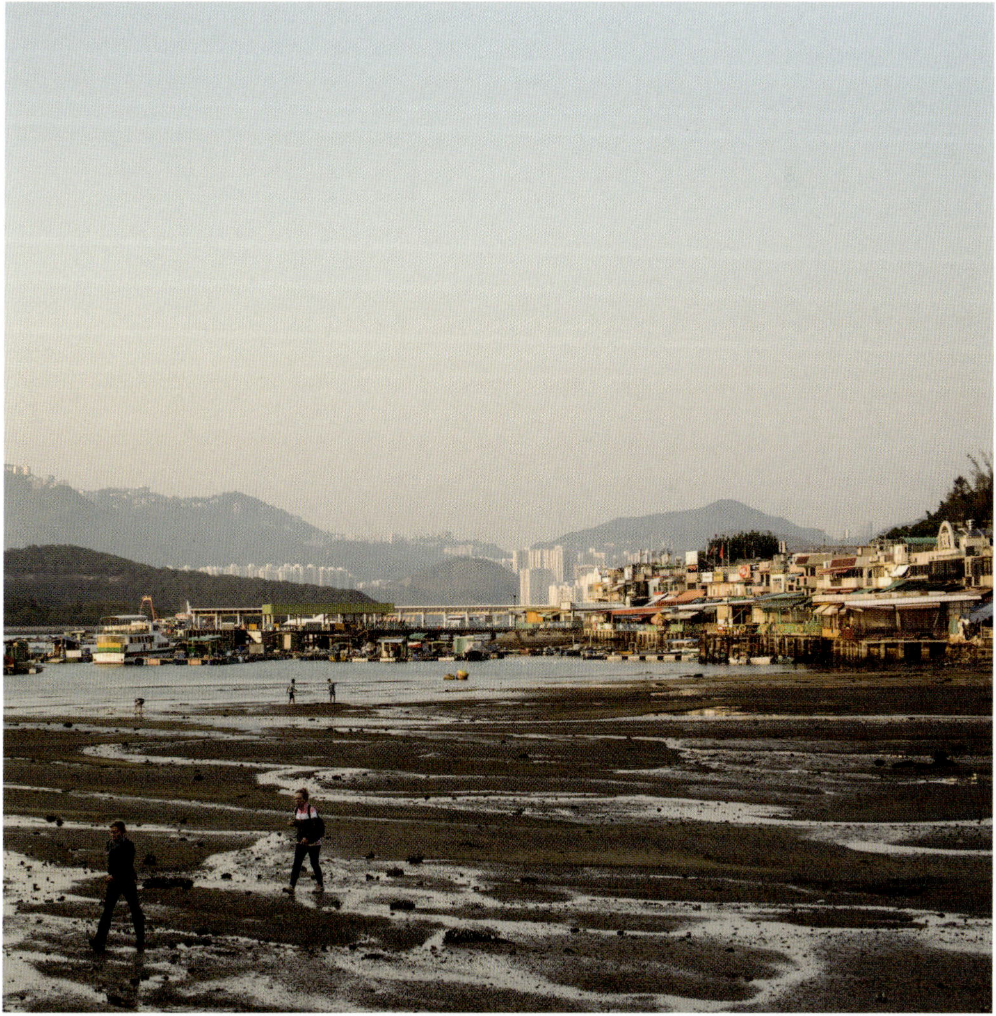

ADVENTURE

# SHEK O

This boho, colourful beach town is pure love. Hard to believe a serene, laidback village like this is just a short taxi ride away from the skyscrapers and hustle of the big city. Avoid weekends on a sunny day, as the beach can get annoyingly packed. Those crowds are hard to blame though, as the sand is clean and golden, the lagoon is clean and the water is calm. Come rent a BBQ pit for a rustic "local" experience (BYO food), have a fancier lunch at one of two beachfront venues: Black Sheep and Cococabana, or stroll the 2.5 maze-like streets of the village to discover your own "secret" dining spot.

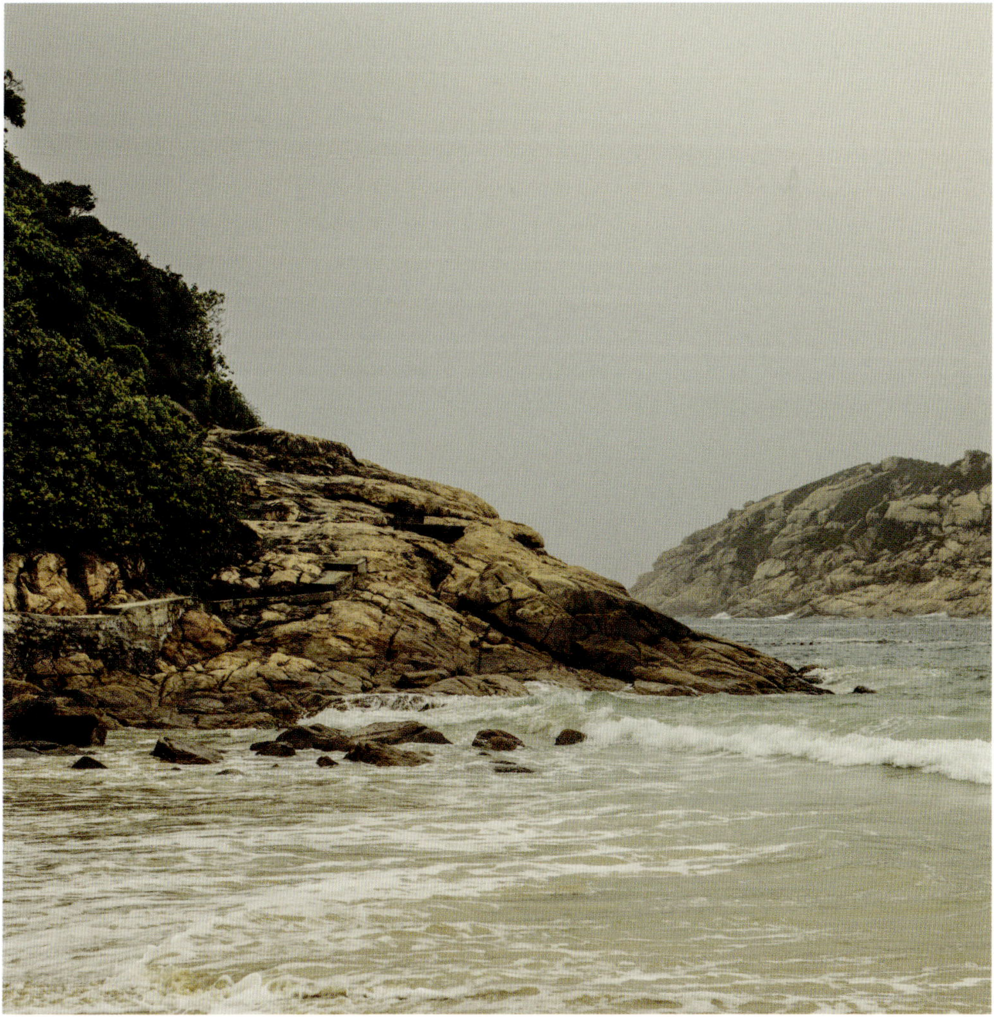

ADVENTURE

EVERYWHERE IN HONG KONG

# HELICOPTER TOUR

You think Victoria Peak is the best – meaning, highest - spot to observe the vertical jungle of the city? Jump into the shiny heli and let Hong Kong WOW you to the extreme. No, seriously: have your James Bond moment. This city is worth it!

www.heliservices.com.hk

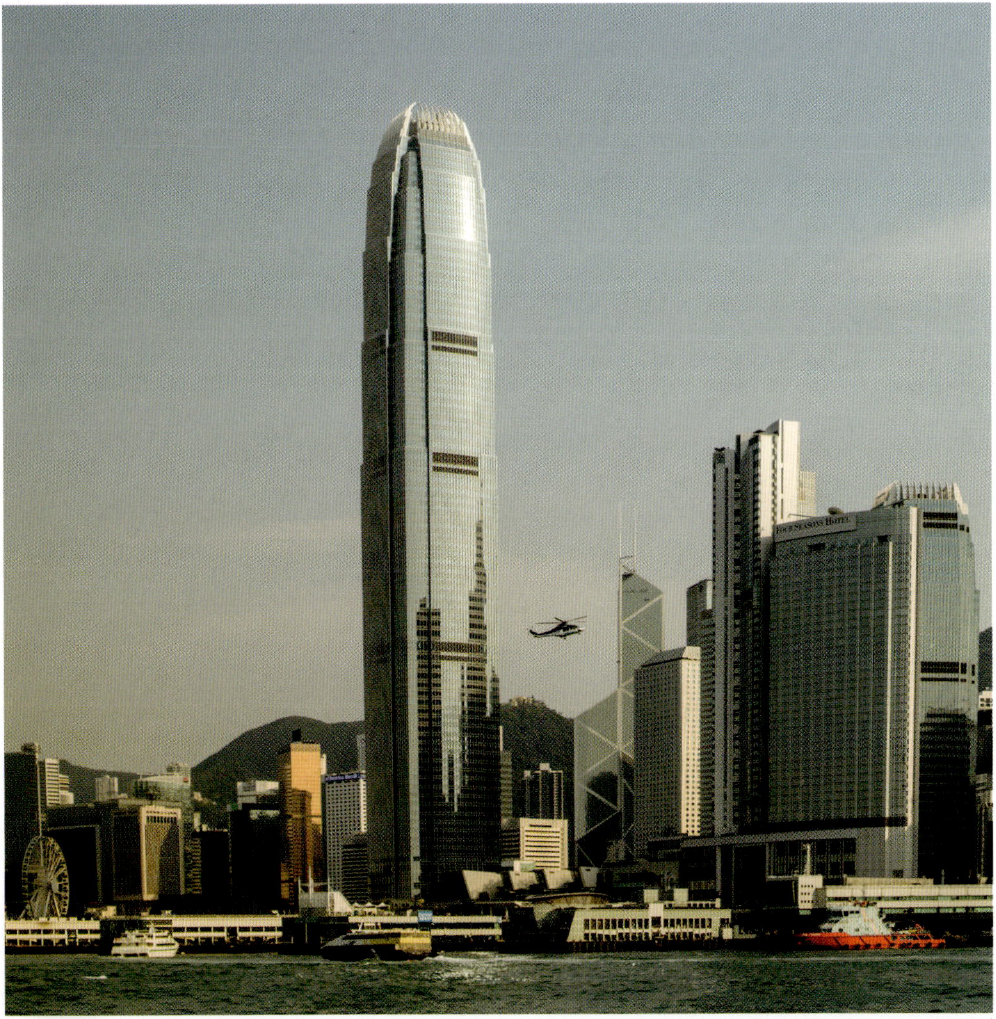

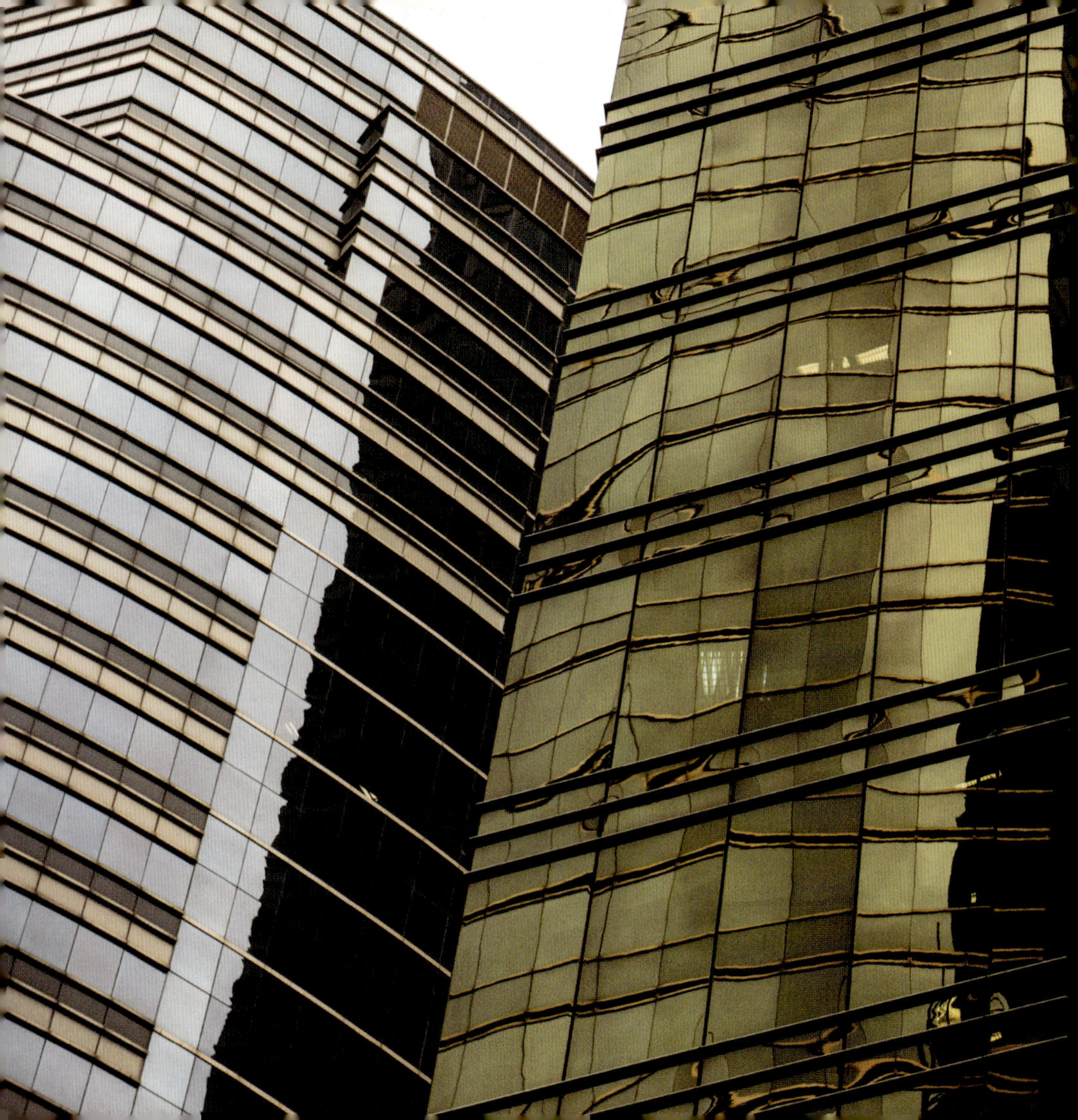

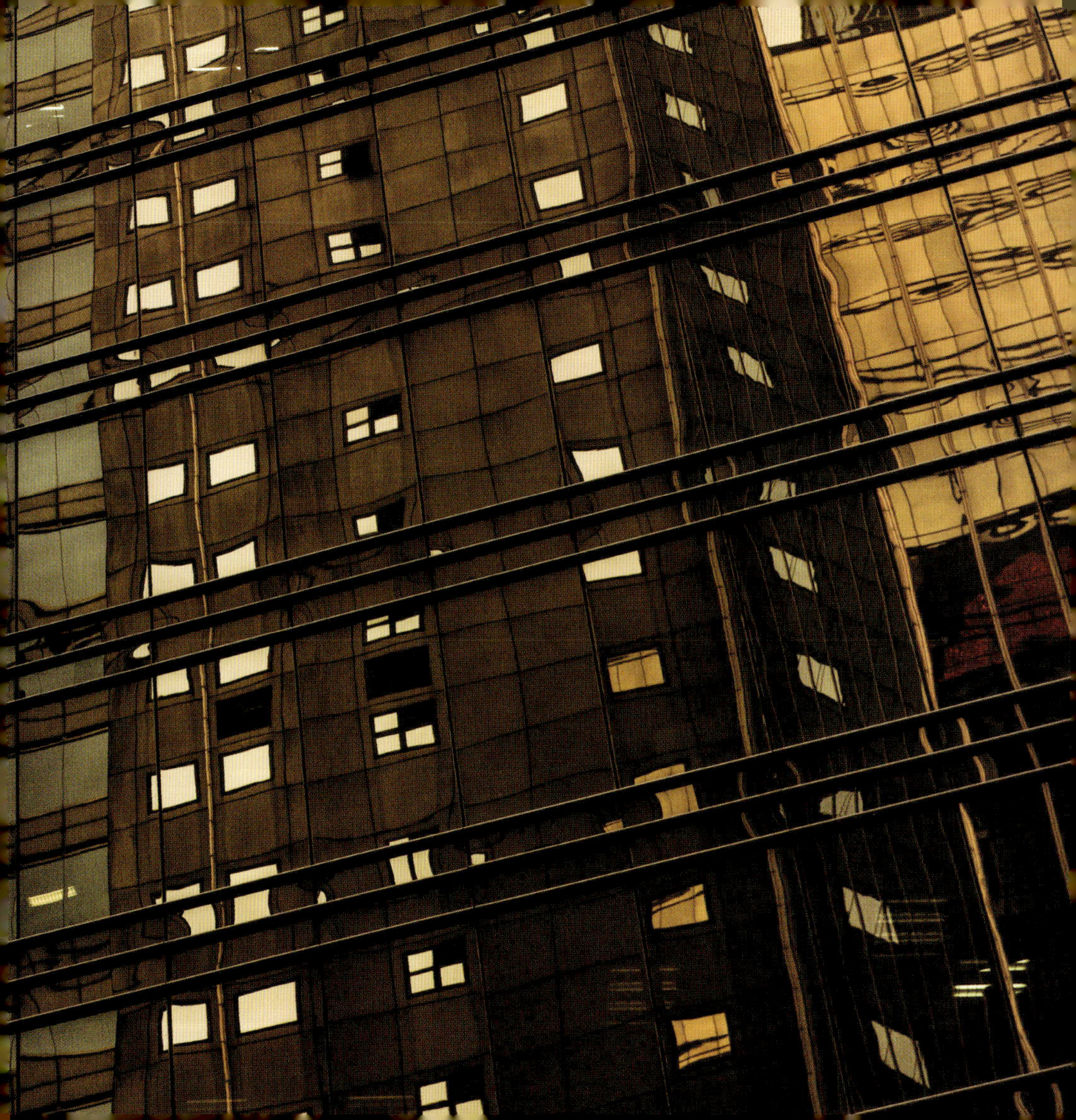

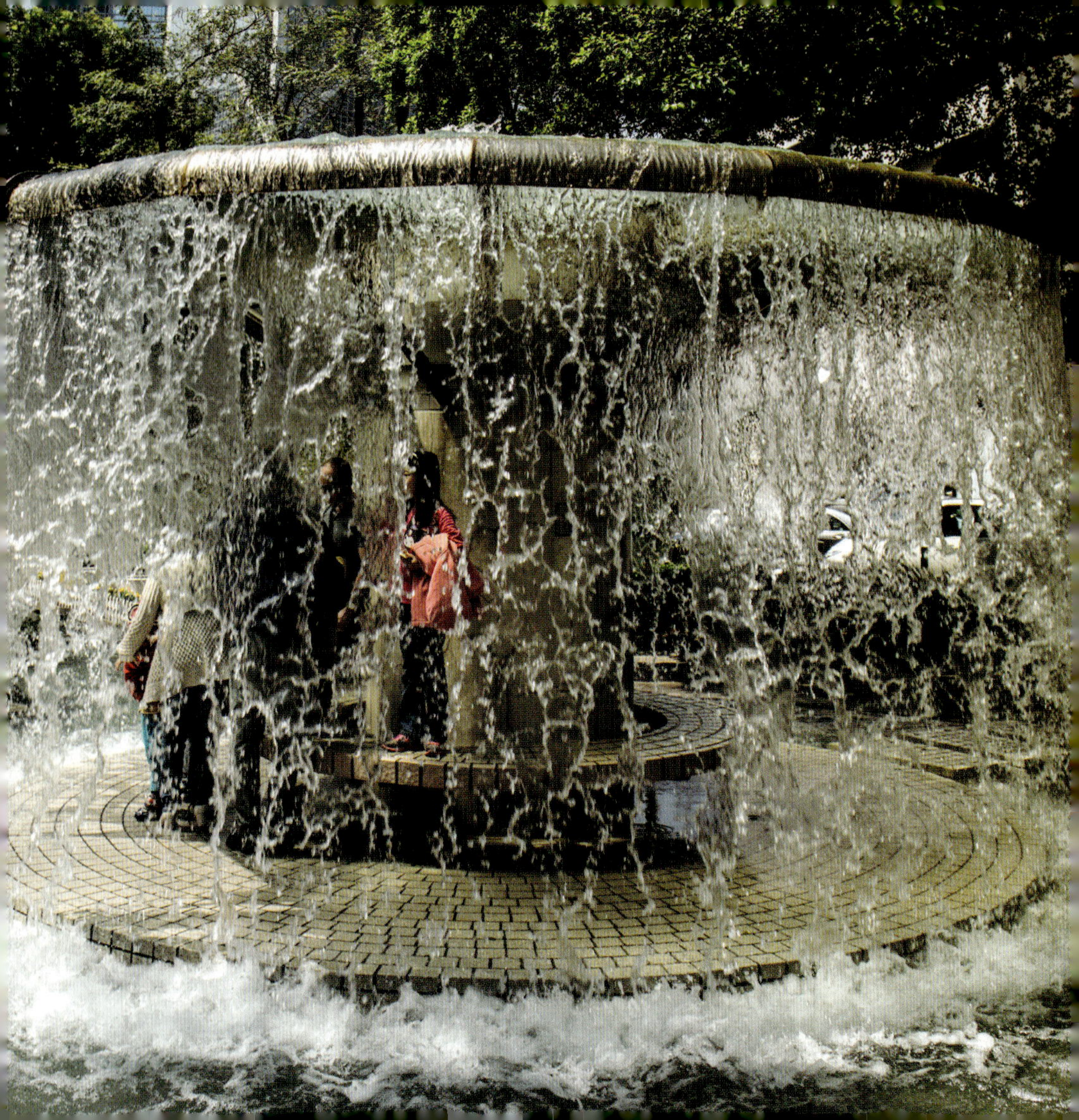

Thank you!

We are extremely grateful to all businesses and entrepreneurs featured in this book - for making Hong Kong the city it is. We have endless admiration for your courage, your passion, your desire to be different, to be unique.

Thank you for making this world a better place!

Veronika Blomgren
Nikola Kostic

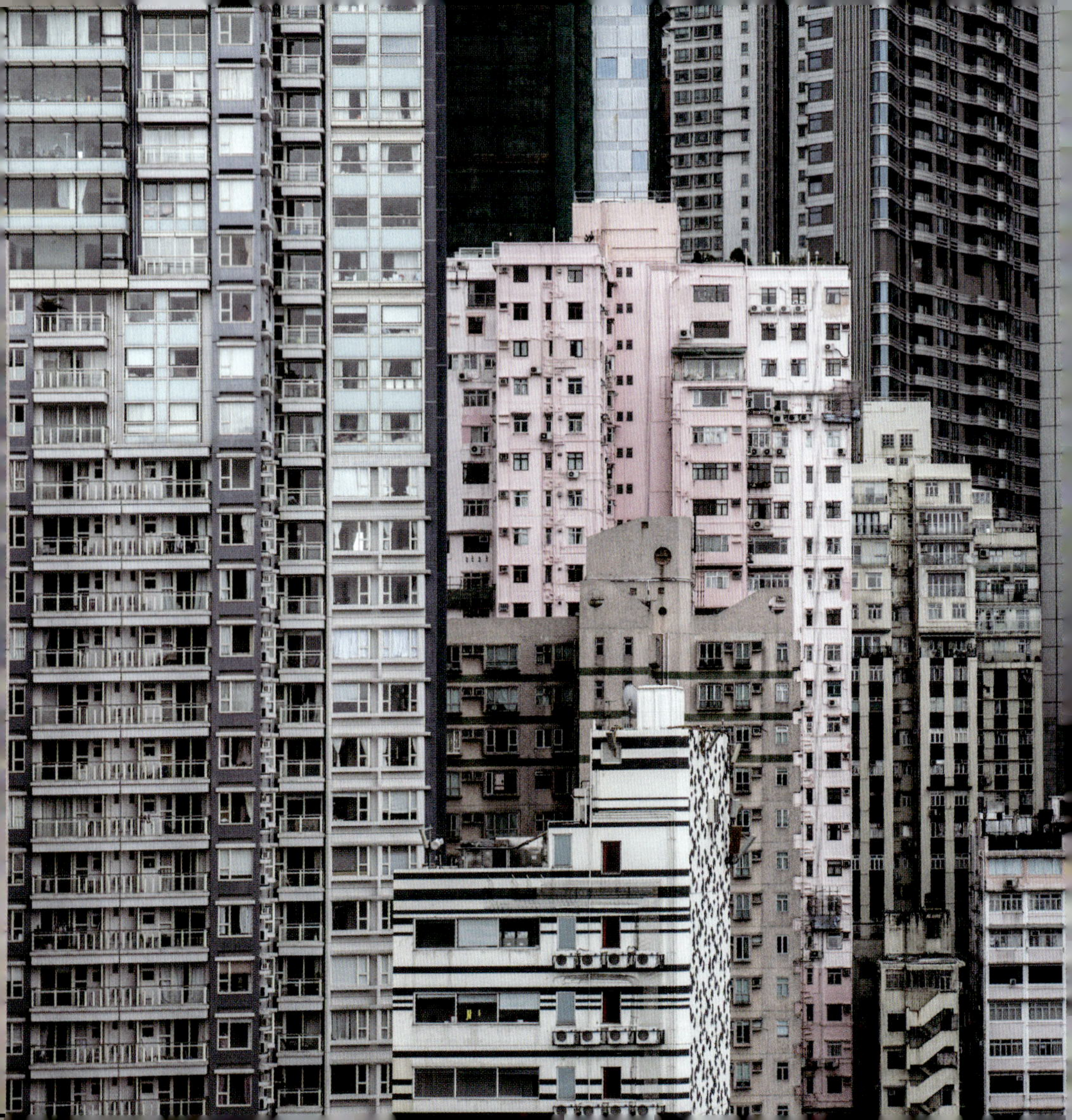

Your recommendations are welcome!

DEFINE FINE is our personal, private collection, and as such it is ever-growing. Please, let us know if we missed a great place or a new one has just opened, if you know a great artist, who will be happy to open his or her world to the public, or someone finally organizes sightseeing tours on flying unicorns (looking forward to that one!).

Please note, that we cannot feature seasonal or short lasting projects – places and people in our collection have to stick around for a while.

Looking forward to hear from you!
www.definefine.com

## SO, HOW DO WE DEFINE WHAT IS "FINE"?

The places we choose for our Define Fine collections are:

BEAUTIFUL. We do believe that beauty will save the world. We are looking for beauty in all of its manifestations.

LOCAL. The places we choose are deeply connected to the quintessence of the local life. We will not recommend a sushi bar in Rome or a pizzeria in Tokyo – unless of course they are incredibly exceptional.

GENUINE. We choose the places that have integrity and where passion is more important than business revenues. Some venues exist only because their owners are quirky and just a little bit crazy. Some swim against the current. But if it is done through true passion – it inevitably wins our hearts.

UNIQUE. We believe in the inspiration of individuality, the bright light of diversity, the magic in endless possibilities from the seed of a great idea. We admire the courage of those who are ready to risk. We applaud those who want to be different.

TOUCHING OUR HEARTS. In our journeys, we are looking for the soul of the cities we visit. We listen to the drums of each city's heartbeat, to the flutes of its streets and we hear the symphony that each city is playing. The places we choose are essential instruments in this orchestra.

## THIS IS HOW WE MAKE OUR DEFINE FINE CITY GUIDES.

We ask the locals. We follow their footsteps.

We listen to our hearts. We trust our judgement.

We never set up a meeting or a photoshoot.

Our opinions are not influenced by anyone.

Our photographs are never pre-arranged.

We come incognito.

We pay our bills.

We love what we do. And we love to share it with you!

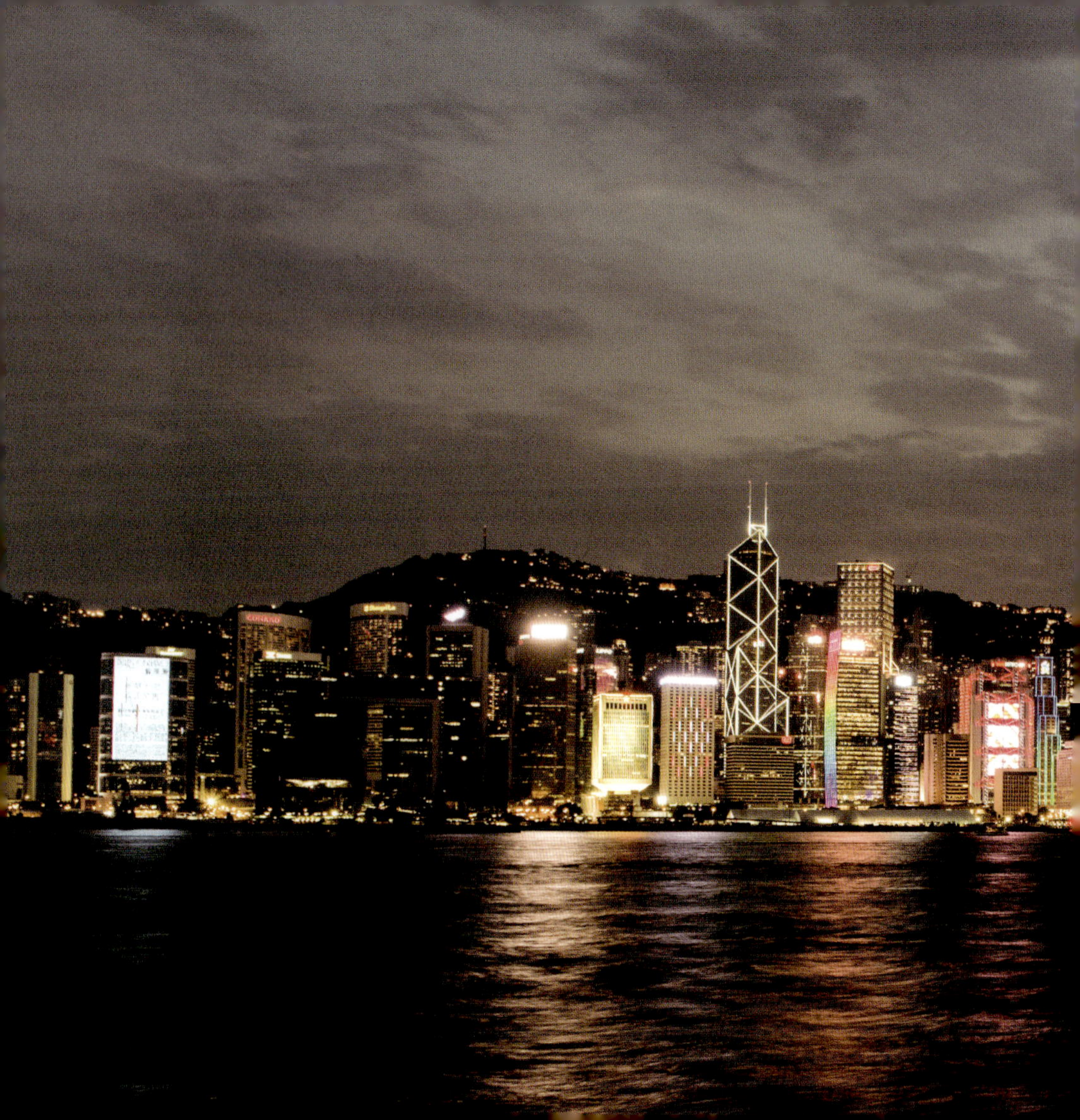

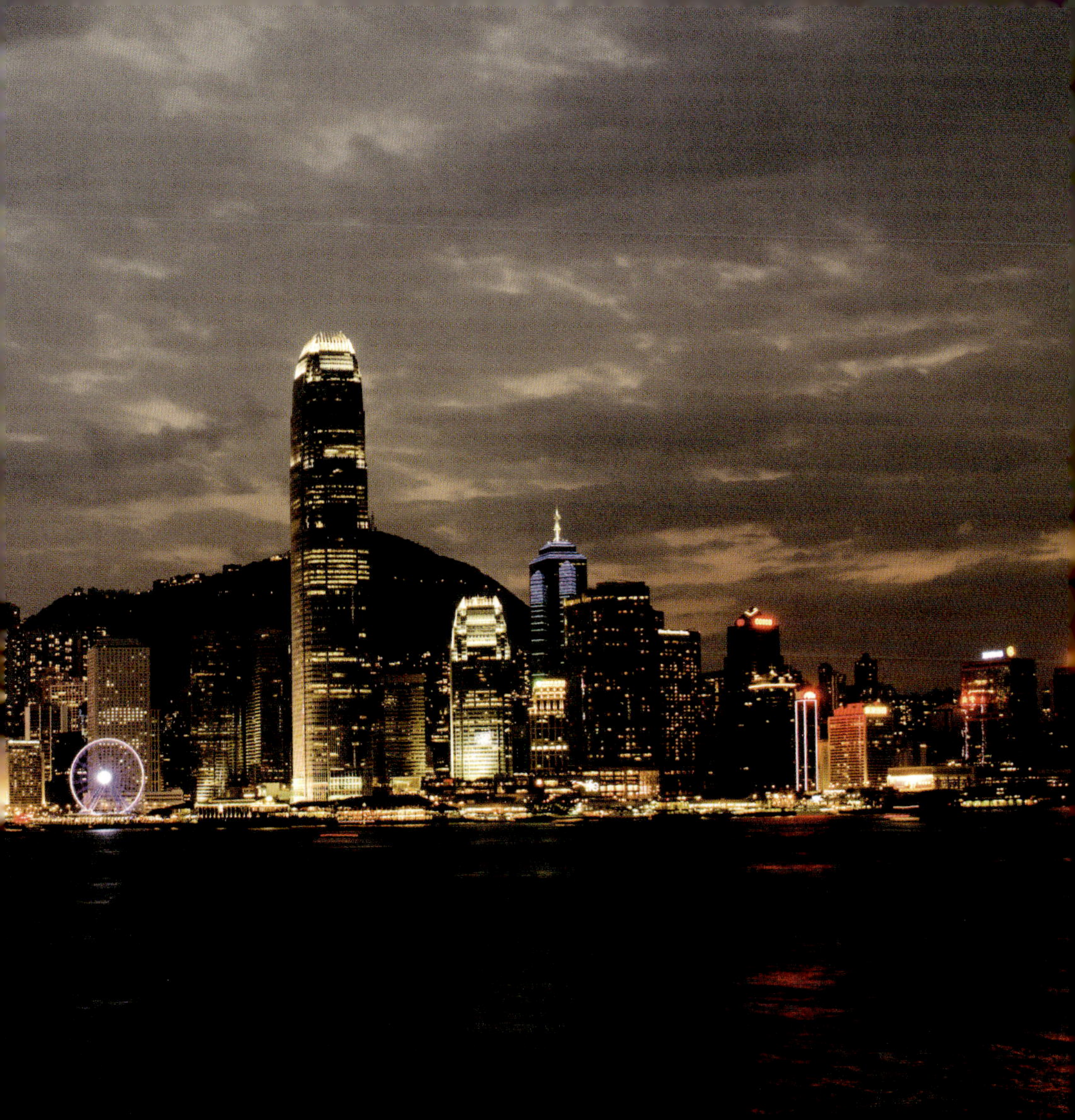

Photography: NIKOLA KOSTIC

Text: MARIA MOZOLEVSKAYA

Graphic Design: NATASHA RADOSAVLJEVIC and NIKOLA KOSTIC

Art Director: VERONIKA BLOMGREN

Research and preproduction: ALEXANDER BLOMGREN

Text editing: SUZANNE KIRALY

Special thanks to GLEN WATSON for great recommendations.

First published in 2016

Publisher DEFINE FINE
www.definefine.com

©2016 Define Fine All rights reserved

No part of this publication may be copied, stored in a retrieval system, or transmitted in any form or by any means, mechanical, photocopying, electronic – without written permission of the publisher.

All the material presented in DEFINE FINE HONG KONG is personal opinion of the authors. The Publisher gives no warranty on accuracy of the content, and to maximum extent, disclaims all liability arising from the use of this publication.

Printed in China

ISBN 978-91-88457-07-3